LUMINOL THEORY

Fig. 1. Hieronymus Bosch, *Ship of Fools* (1490–1500)

First published in 2017 by punctum books, Earth, Milky Way.
https://punctumbooks.com

ISBN-13: 978-1-947447-12-7 (print); 978-1-947447-13-4 (ePDF)

LCCN: 2017951816
Library of Congress Cataloging Data is available from the Library of Congress

Editing: Athena Tan
Book design: Vincent W.J. van Gerven Oei

HIC SVNT MONSTRA

Laura E. Joyce

LUMINOL THEORY

For Naomi and Tom

Acknowledgments

Enormous thanks to Rachel O'Connell for giving me the confidence and ability to finish this project. Special thanks to Diarmuid Hester and Tom Houlton for their important late interventions on this manuscript. Thanks, also, to Sam Solomon for his wisdom and guidance. Thanks to Joyelle McSweeney for her inspirational theory-poetics and for her guidance and support. This manuscript would not have been possible without the careful feedback and ongoing support of Naomi Booth, Camilla Bostock, Tom Bunstead, Alys Conran, Kieran Devaney, Dulcie Few, Helen Jukes, Jodie Kim, Thomas Joyce, Kathryn Pallant, and Nicholas Royle.

This project would not have been possible without the inspiring work on *The Shining* and its afterlives by Mark Fisher and Leyland Kirby (The Caretaker). I would also like to thank Johannes Göransson and Olivia Cronk for their poetry, their generous interviews, and their support for this project.

I am extremely grateful to Athena Tan for the care that she took with my manuscript and the opportunity that she gave me to work on improving the book.

I cannot express how grateful I am to Vincent W.J. van Gerven Oei and Eileen Joy for the dedication and support that I have received whilst working on this project. Thank you.

Thank you to Rebecca Devaney for being the creepiest and best muse.

Contents

Figure 1. Girl in the basement. Still from *The Luminol Reels*.

Preface

Hereisthehouseitisgreenandwhiteithasareddooritis-
veryprettyhereisthefamilymotherfatherdickandjane-
liveinthegreenandwhitehousetheyareveryhappy
— Toni Morrison, *The Bluest Eye*

Christmas, Colorado, 1996

On Christmas Day, 1996, JonBenét Ramsey was reported missing by her family. JonBenét was six years old; she was also a successful child beauty queen. Patricia Ramsey, JonBenét's mother, claimed to have discovered a ransom note left on the stairs of their home that apparently alerted the family to the fact that her daughter was missing. Though the note specifically indicated that JonBenét had been abducted, her father, John Ramsey, began the search for his daughter with two of his friends *starting in the basement*. Specifically, they looked in the area of the basement that was used as a wine cellar. They very quickly discovered the body of JonBenét, a factor considered highly suspicious by the police and at odds with the information in the ransom note that indicated she had been removed from the house. At once, the basement became a crime scene.

The basement is a staple of horror narratives, and Bernice M. Murphy draws on Gaston Bachelard's seminal architectural work *The Poetics of Space* when she describes the "suburban basement" as "frequently a place in which unspeakable horrors lurk in the modern horror film."[1] She argues:

As Gaston Bachelard noted of the symbolic significance of cellars, the space is "first and foremost the *dark entity* of the house, the one that partakes of subterranean forces. When we dream there, we are in harmony with the irrationality of the depths." Similarly, basements in the Suburban Gothic are invariably associated with murder, the concealment of terrible crimes and illicit burial.[2]

When JonBenét was discovered in the basement of the Ramsey home she became part of an overarching Suburban Gothic

1 Gaston Bachelard, *The Poetics of Space,* trans. Maria Jolas (1964; New York: Penguin Classics, 2014); Bernice M. Murphy, *The Suburban Gothic in American Popular Culture* (Basingstoke: Palgrave, 2009), 154–55.

2 Murphy, *The Suburban Gothic in American Popular Culture,* 154–55.

narrative. The fact that her murder remains unsolved in spite of mass media coverage and extensive expert forensic analysis means that she has passed into the realm of myth and folklore; she is a truly haunting figure. The basement "conceals" the terrible crime of her murder temporarily until she is discovered, but on a more profound level, the basement conceals the crime forever. The evidence discovered there is illegible; the basement will not reveal the secret of JonBenét's "illicit burial."

Aside from the strangeness of the basement search, two other major discrepancies have never been accounted for in the case, and each of them has the quality of a myth or a nightmare. The first, and most widely reported, is the case of the missing footprints. The murder took place in the depths of a Colorado winter, when snow lay deep on the ground; yet there were no traces of footprints. This initially gave rise to intense speculation that the crime must have been committed inside the house, and the case became a true-crime locked-room mystery. Later, investigative reporter Julie Hayden looked more closely at footage of the snowbound house and reported:

> We looked at the videotape once the footprints in the snow started becoming an issue and one of the things that I observed was, there did not seem to be snow going up to all of the doors. So, in my opinion, this thing about footprints in the snow has always been much ado about nothing because it seemed clear to me that people could have gotten in the house, whether they did or not, without traipsing through the snow.[3]

This analysis punctures the hermetically sealed mystery by allowing for multiple narratives. Hayden shatters the story into fragments by arguing that "people could have gotten in the house, whether they did or not, without traipsing through the

---

3   "Jonbenet Ramsey: Who Killed Jonbenet," Mills Productions, Channel 4, 1998. http://www.millsproductions.co.uk/jonbenet-ramsey/who-killed-jonbenet.shtml

snow." Here Hayden replaces the suspicious reading with an excavatory one, indicating multiple unhierarchized strata. As the crime could have occurred within or without the Ramsey house, there is no single legible narrative. This crime scene is not sealed, is not alien, but rather is part of a wider, cultural site of violence.

A second piece of evidence that caused widespread confusion, and at one juncture seemed to point to JonBenét's murder within the home, was a dish of pineapple found in the kitchen of which she had eaten a portion:

> For many years, the general public had heard that pineapple had been found in JBR's small intestine. [...] A bowl of pineapple was found in the breakfast area off from the kitchen [...]. It seems implausible that a stranger or acquaintance intruder would have had the motivation or ability to get JBR to eat pineapple on her way to being assaulted. [...] It is more plausible to imagine a "friendly" intruder, e.g., in the guise of a "secret visit" from Santa, having the motivation and means to do this, albeit a "diversion" that would have elevated the risk of being caught by the parents or Burke while in the kitchen or dining area.[4]

The dish of pineapple is abandoned on the work surface, an artifact at the scene. This clue is deeply unsettling; tinned tropical fruit is transformed from a Christmas treat into gustatory evidence within JonBenét's body. The disjunction between the apparent homeliness of the Ramseys' Christmas Day and the violence of JonBenét's death is uncanny. Whether or not this speculative scene has any truth in it (the intruder offering Jon-Benét a last meal; a murderous Santa), there is a rupture within the home. The regularity and banality of meal times is compromised and becomes sinister. No member of the Ramsey fam-

---

4   "The Pineapple Evidence," *JonBenét Ramsey Case Encyclopedia*, http://jonbenetramsey.pbworks.com/w/page/11682517/The%20Pineapple%20Evidence.

ily claims to have any knowledge of the pineapple, and this fact signals a break in the smooth running of the household. At best the six-year-old JonBenét was left fending for herself, or looking to an intruder to meet her dietary needs; at worst the family was lying to cover up her murder.

D.A. Miller argues in his book *The Novel and the Police* that the happy family is simply a facet of the disciplinary institution, exerting control over the time, activities, and basic needs of the individual.[5] The Ramsey home can be seen as an instantiation of this disciplinary unit, with the family basement as the ultimate site of corporal discipline — a site that John Ramsey, JonBenét's father, is instinctively drawn towards. Aside from the obvious psychoanalytic reading of the basement as the unconscious, there is also a socioeconomic reading of the basement as an indicator of wealth. A basement generally belongs to a large building that has several unnecessary rooms; in the Ramseys' case this included the added luxury of a wine cellar. In conjunction with the central crime of murder, the Ramsey basement can be read palimpsestically as a space for the capitalist accumulation of wealth and the colonization of land — both staples of the American Gothic narrative.

The most acute subgenre of the American Gothic narrative is perhaps that of Suburban Gothic, a term coined by Bernice Murphy, as mentioned above. This subgenre takes place in domestic locations, where the uniformity of the suburbs is an uncanny indicator of the inhuman. In this subgenre, larger colonial and genocidal forces are explicated through violent crimes against the individual. Arthur Kroker, a scholar of Suburban Gothic, suggests that the very sameness of the suburbs is "sinister":

> Most of all, it is the lawns which are sinister. Fuji green and expansive, they are a visual relief to the freeway and its accompanying tunnel vision. Even ahead of the golden arches, they are welcoming as the approach of a new urban sign-

---

5   D.A. Miller, *The Novel and the Police* (Berkeley: University of California Press, 1988), 10.

value. The frenzy sites of a decaying Christian culture where reclining lawn chairs, people in the sun, barbecues and summer-time swimming pools can give off the pleasant odors of an imploding Calvinist culture, playing psychologically at the edge of the parasite and the predator.[6]

Kroker is describing the context of late capitalism, of the postwar United States, and of urban sprawl cutting into the countryside. The banal multiplicity of the suburbs, built on material obsession and replete with replicas of nature, is horrifying and repellent to Kroker, who frames the suburbs within a religious paradigm. His "frenzy sites of a decaying Christian culture," with its implicit hysterical decadence, could be applied as easily to the opening of the first millennium as to the US in the early twentieth century.[7] The numinous nature of the hypergreen lawns of suburban North America are a façade for a culture in "frenzy" and "implo[sion]." Commenting on Kroker's work, Kim Ian Michasiw also reads contamination, disease, and disgust in the "unnaturally vigorous turf" and asks whether "something might ooze from us and fuse us with the lawn."[8] These references to the "unnatural" greenness of the "turf" and the notion of "fus[ing] with the lawn" are indicators of palimpsestic saturation. There is no escape from the contaminative traces of suburban horror, no escape from the crime scene.

6 Arthur Kroker, *Panic Encyclopedia* (New York: St. Martin's Press, 1989), 211–12.

7 In his 1998 work *Tales from Ovid,* which translates Ovid's Metamorphoses, Ted Hughes makes an explicit comparison between the Augustan empire — it was flooded with "ecstatic cults" and at "sea in hysteria and despair" — and the end of the twentieth century. He says of Ovid's tales that they "establish a rough register of what it feels like to live in the psychological gulf that opens up at the end of an era. Among everything else that we see in them, we certainly recognise this." Ted Hughes, *Tales from Ovid: Twenty-Four Passages from the "Metamorphoses"* (London: Faber & Faber, 1997), 6.

8 Kim Ian Michasiw, "Some Stations of Suburban Gothic," in *American Gothic: New Interventions in a National Narrative,* eds. Robert K. Martin and Eric Savoy (Iowa City: University of Iowa Press, 1998), 246.

The lawns glow unnaturally luminol green.

Figure 2. Queer Light. Still from *The Luminol Reels*.

Queer Light
Forensics, Psychoanalysis, Hermeneutics

*Fausak had never experienced anything like it. He felt as if he
were in a sci-fi movie. Initially, there was the same pale green
light. It got greener and brighter. It began to glow. And through
its luminosity he could see the trail of blood. The trail was solid,
but with streaks in it, as though someone had taken a big wet
mop and wrung it out and dragged it along the floor. The length
of the bloody trail measured some 55 feet. The shimmering glow
hung in the air, above Fausak's knees. It had become so bright
that he could see the faces of the forensic men and the chemists.*
— Peter Maas, *In a Child's Name:
The Legacy of a Mother's Murder*

1. Forensics

When human blood reacts with luminol it lights up a ghostly blue-green. Most commonly used to detect whether violence has taken place at suspected crime scenes, this reaction combines the human and the chemical in a moment of violent transformation. According to Stuart H. James and William G. Eckert's *Interpretation of Bloodstain Evidence at Crime Scenes,* luminol is a chemical that "produces a bright luminescence when in the presence of the most minute amounts of blood."[1] There is a long and fascinating history of the application of luminol in crime-scene analysis. A.J. Schmitz is cited as the first chemist to synthesize luminol, in 1902, though James and Eckert claim that "a paper by Gill states luminol's discovery to be around 1853."[2] The term *luminol* was, in fact, coined by chemists Ernest Huntress, Lester Stanley, and Almon Parker in their 1934 paper, "The Preparation of 3-Aminophthalhydrazide for Use in the Demonstration of Chemiluminescence."[3] James and Eckert offer a gloss on the paper:

> Chemiluminescence occurs when a molecule capable of fluorescing is raised to an excited level during a chemical reaction. Upon its return to the ground state energy in the form of light is emitted. Only a few molecules are known to emit appreciable amounts of light, and of those, luminol is one of the most outstanding.[4]

Essentially, the reaction between two chemicals (in this case, blood and luminol) causes the "molecule capable of fluorescing"

---

1   Stuart H. James and William G. Eckert, *Interpretation of Bloodstain Evidence at Crime Scenes,* 2nd ed. (Boca Raton: CRC Press, 1998), 159.

2   Ibid., 159–60.

3   Ernest Huntress, Lester Stanley, and Almon Parker, "The Preparation of 3-Aminophthalhydrazide for Use in the Demonstration of Chemiluminescence," *Journal of the American Chemical Society* 56, no. 1 (1934): 241–42.

4   James and Eckert, *Interpretation of Bloodstain Evidence at Crime Scenes,* 160.

(i.e., luminol) to become "excited": a state of transformation, of reaction. According to Kenneth L. Williamson:

Oxidation of luminol is attended with a striking emission of blue-green light. An alkaline solution of the compound is allowed to react with a mixture of hydrogen peroxide and potassium ferricyanide. The dianion (5) is oxidised to the triplet excited state (two unpaired electrons of like spin) (6) of the amino phthalate ion (Scheme 2). This slowly undergoes intersystem crossing to the singlet excited state (two unpaired electrons of opposite spin) (7), which decays to the ground state ion (8) with the emission of one quantum of light (a photon) per molecule.[5]

When this reaction is complete, luminol returns to "ground level" and the excess energy that has been created during the reaction is expressed as luminescence, as light.[6] There is no direct explanation in the article as to why Huntress, Stanley, and Parker chose the name *luminol,* though the word has close etymological associations with other words relating to light. There are several etymologically similar words in the 2016 Oxford

---

5   Kenneth L. Williamson, *Macroscale and Microscale Organic Experiments,* 4th ed. (Boston: Houghton Mifflin, 2005).

6   For more on luminol, see James and Weckert, *Interpretation of Bloodstain Evidence at Crime Scenes,* 15–156, particularly the reference list at the end of the chapter. Particularly useful sources include: H.O. Albrecht, "Über die Chemiluminescenz des Aminophthalaurehydrazids," *Zeitschrift für Physikalische Chemie* 136 (1928): 321–30; R.R.J. Grispino, "The Effect of Luminol on the Serological Analysis of Dried Human Bloodstains," *Crime Laboratory Digest* 17, no. 1 (1990): 13–23; Huntress, Stanley, and Parker, "Preparation of 3-Aminophthalhydrazide"; D.L. Laux, "Effects of Luminol on the Subsequent Analysis of Bloodstains," *Journal of Forensic Sciences* 36, no. 5 (1991): 1512–20; J. McGrath, "The Chemical Luminescence Test for Blood," *British Medical Journal* 2 (1942): 156–57; W. Specht, "The Chemiluminescence of Hemin: An Aid for Finding and Recognizing Blood Stains Important for Forensic Purposes," *Angewante Chemie* 50 (1937): 155–57; John I. Thornton and Ralph S. Maloney, "The Chemistry of the Luminol Reaction: Where To from Here?," *California Association of Criminalists Newsletter,* September 1985, 9–17.

English Dictionary: *luminous* (a. Full of light; emitting or casting light; shining, bright; b. Of a room: Well lighted; c. applied to animals or plants which emit light), *illuminate* (a. To light up, give light to; b. Light to, or remove blindness from [the eyes], esp. fig. in religious sense), and *luna* (1. The moon personified; 2a. Alchemy. Silver).[7]

These etymological roots are mainly concerned with light, and it is this chemiluminescent aspect of 3-aminophthalhydrazide that the term *luminol* appears to foreground. But there are also sacred resonances (the personified moon; religious enlightenment) and even magical or miraculous overtones (removing blindness; alchemy). Luminol is assonant with *liminal* ("of or relating to a limen, relating to the point beyond which a sensation becomes too faint to be experienced"[8]), a term that describes the excavated, ghostly narratives that are revealed through the application of luminol.

Finally, the term *limn,* bound etymologically to *liminal,* as well as to *illuminate* and *luminous,* describes the process of "lay[ing] on," "adorn[ing]," or "embellish[ing] with gold or bright colour," with particular reference to religious manuscripts in order to (literally) highlight important passages.[9] The term *limn* is a useful way of thinking about luminol theory as the word combines two of the meanings of *luminol*: first, the process of chemiluminescence, the "laying on" of "bright colour" to palimpsestically reveal hidden narratives; second, the annotative function of limning manuscripts allows for a careful editor to present a series of margin notes, a narrative in fragments, that can be clearly understood. Luminol theory is a textual reading strategy that mimics the excavatory, illuminating function of luminol analysis. Like luminol, the theory operates by illuminating in flashes. It requires deep thought and careful interpretation on the part of the analyst, who excavates from the known to the unknown to piece together a wider narrative.

---

7   *Oxford English Dictionary,* s.vv. "luminous," "illuminate," "luna."

8   Ibid., s.v. "liminal."

9   Ibid., s.v. "limn."

Luminol theory operates especially successfully when pairing texts with their chronological moment in forensic history. Though genre fiction, particularly crime and thriller stories, have long been concerned with forensic science, and though there already exist many novels, films, and television shows that exploit this trope, there is not yet a textual reading strategy that applies the metaphorical use of luminol to read a range of cultural texts. The history of luminol and the development of the forensic sciences have informed the choices of primary texts to be read, or excavated, in this book. The case study of Jon-Benét Ramsey is particularly relevant, having occurred in the mid-1990s, a very specific time in the rise of forensic science: just as investigators and the legal system were beginning to take forensic analysis seriously, but on the cusp of the 2000s, when further research would cast doubt on its accuracy and efficacy and demonstrate that it was possible to prove that DNA evidence could be fabricated.[10]

The Ramsey case is at the heart of the North American cultural imaginary, and it resonates within the history of forensic science in the United States. The American Academy of Forensic Sciences (AAFS), the foremost institute for the study of fo-

---

10 In 1995 the Federal Bureau of Investigation (FBI) launched the Combined DNA Index System, which became possible due to the DNA Identification Act of 1994 (42 U. S. C. § 14132). "Combined DNA Index System," FBI, https://www.fbi.gov/about-us/lab/biometric-analysis/codis/combined-dna-index-system%20. On the fabrication of DNA and other forensic evidence, see Andrew Pollack, "DNA Evidence Can Be Fabricated, Scientists Show," *New York Times*, August 17, 2009, http://www.nytimes.com/2009/08/18/science/18dna.html; and Radley Balko, "A Brief History of Forensics," *Washington Post*, April 21, 2015, http://www.washingtonpost.com/news/the-watch/wp/2015/04/21/a-brief-history-of-forensics/. It is interesting to note that forensic anthropology also benefited from advances in DNA technologies. A group known as the EAAF (Argentine Forensic Anthropology Team, http://www.eaaf.org/) was set up in Argentina in the mid-1980s to "investigate the cases of at least 9,000 disappeared people in Argentina under the military government that ruled from 1976 to 1983." This rendering visible of the "disappeared" dead is analogous to the project of this book: to shine a light on forensic evidence in order to make visible, and central, the missing dead.

rensic science in the country, was founded in Colorado in 1948. The founding of the academy foreshadows the Ramsey case by taking place in the same state as the murder and because two of its most prominent members, Henry Lee and Gerald R. McMenamin, would rise to fame partly as a result of their work on the Ramsey case. McMenamin evaluated the ransom note that was found in the Ramsey home hours before the body of JonBenét was discovered in the basement and included his analysis as a case study in his influential 2002 book *Forensic Linguistics: Advances in Forensic Stylistics.*[11]

The earliest rise in forensic analysis, even before the AAFS was founded, was contemporaneous with the emergence of eugenics and its conception of purity. *Purity,* an idea that is perfectly functional when dealing with the possibility of contamination at the crime scene, was popularized as a racist euphemism by Francis Galton, pioneer of both eugenics and forensic technologies. One of the earliest practitioners of fingerprinting, Galton served the police state in ideological as well as practical ways.[12] His manifesto on eugenics contains the following: "The community might be trusted to refuse representatives of criminals, and

---

11 McMenamin was asked to rule out that the note had been written by either of JonBenét's parents. He had great faith in his findings; in the section of the case study on limitations, he was confident enough to state: "With respect to the possibility of attempted disguise, manipulation of the non request, precrime samples in the known Ramsey reference writings was not possible. Additionally, most variables identified in the Ramseys' request writings, in writings used here to exclude the Ramseys as writers of the ransom letter and in those not used (e.g., dictated word lists), contain such a patterned level of consistency that the conscious manipulation of even the most carefully executed request writings is highly improbable, given the circumstances of their production." Gerald R. McMenamin, *Forensic Linguistics: Advances in Forensic Stylistics* (Boca Raton: CRC Press, 2002), 4.

12 Francis Galton, *Finger Prints* (1892; Amherst: Prometheus Books, 2006), 219. See also Francis Galton, *Essays in Eugenics,* 3rd ed. (1909; CreateSpace Independent Publishing Platform, 2013); "The Francis Galton Papers," *Wellcome Library,* http://wellcomelibrary.org/collections/digital-collections/makers-of-modern-genetics/digitised-archives/francis-galton/.

of others that it rates as undesirable."[13] This conflation between criminality and undesirability is slippery and problematic. The statement also raises the question of who gets to be "the community" and who is classed as "undesirable." Galton clarifies this distinction and makes his racism explicit by claiming, "While most barbarous races disappear, some, like the negro, do not."[14] His call for a racist and genocidal eugenics was evangelical in nature, and he proselytised that the pseudoscience "must be introduced into the national conscience, like a new religion. It has, indeed, strong claims to be an orthodox religious tenet of the future, for eugenics co-operate with the workings of nature by securing that humanity shall be represented by the fittest races. What nature does blindly, slowly, and ruthlessly, man may do providently, quickly, and kindly."[15] This desire to purify and cleanse imagines a utopia predicated on racial annihilation. A forensic humanities, such as luminol theory, argues that we exist in teeming, bacterial, ecologies and that there is no stasis, no purity: we cannot opt out of the ecologies we are in. Luminol theory argues for a forensic humanities to counteract the ideology of annihilatory purity.

The "kindness" of Galton's suggested program of genocide via forced sterilization is satirized in Michael Du Plessis's 2011 novella *The Memoirs of JonBenet Ramsey by Kathy Acker,*[16] itself a palimpsestic version of Stephen King's 1977 novel *The Shining* and its 1980 film adaptation by Stanley Kubrick. The novella's protagonist, an animated doll version of murdered toddler Jon-Benét Ramsey, reflects on her hometown of Boulder, Colorado, in terms that explicitly reference Galton's manifesto.

---

13 Francis Galton, "Eugenics: Its Definition, Scope, and Aims," *American Journal of Sociology* 10, no. 1 (1904): 2.

14 Ibid.

15 Ibid., 5.

16 Michael Du Plessis, *The Memoirs of JonBenet Ramsey by Kathy Acker* (Los Angeles: Les Figues Press, 2012), hereafter *Memoirs*. According to its website, "Les Figues Press embraces a feminist criticality and editorial vision. [It is] interested in work that is aware of itself as a textual body within a history and culture marked (like physical bodies) by constructs of gender, race, class, and sexuality."

JonBenét Ramsey's basement is important to luminol theory both because of the moment of forensic history that it occupies, and because it is a microcosm of larger, systemic crime scenes. Lying on the limen, or threshold, between mythic and true crime, the basement recurs throughout this book. Traces of luminol illuminate the crime scene and allow a zooming out from the Ramsey basement to the wider setting of Colorado, colonial North America, and beyond. Saturation, radioactivity, and the occult make the crime scene visible, luminous, and endless. JonBenét as absent referent haunts the scene. In *Memoirs,* Du Plessis uses this crime scene to interrogate the broader crime scene of Colorado, and, by extension, the North America built on genocide and eugenics.

Memoirs is an experimental, nested narrative that reimagines the life and death of JonBenét Ramsey, who is first embodied by the writer Kathy Acker and then, in a vision, by an adolescent named Tiffany, who dies of an ecstasy overdose at her sweet-sixteen party.[17] There are also episodes that include Acker lecturing at Boulder University and scenes where JonBenét goes to tea with a male doll named Little Lord Fauntleroy. The status of JonBenét as interstitial ghost child, half adult and half vulnerable toddler, is unsettling and provocative. Perhaps the most bizarre aspect of the novella is the setting: the entirety of Boulder is contained within "an ugly snow globe that someone bought in a cheap airport gift store and stuck […] at the foot of the Rocky Mountains."[18] *Memoirs* exposes harms done and invites the reader to consider their relationship to those harms. Rather than occupying an easy, didactic space where violence and atrocities are othered, this novella reminds us of our complicity:

17 As I will discuss in chapter 3, this name corresponds to that of Tiffany Johnson, a young woman murdered by Matthew Murray at a mass shooting in Arvada, Colorado, in 2007. It is likely that Michael Du Plessis was aware of this shooting which happened in the period when he was researching and writing this novella.

18 Du Plessis, *Memoirs,* 3.

Boulder: where eugenics couples with software to secure the reproduction of middle-class bodies, bodies that desire only perfect reproduction. Boulder: where white-collar heaven beckons under pitiless white-collar skies. Boulder: where cotton-ball, cotton-candy cirri hang over the Flatirons like the prettiest, freshest mushroom clouds ever.[19]

In Du Plessis's version of Boulder, the ostensibly sweet and pretty town is secretly decaying. Kathy Acker/JonBenét says of her childhood self: "In her dream, the town was a repository of all her dreams. A town that was always decaying. In the centre of this town her father had hanged himself."[20] This version of Boulder as experienced by the fragmented narrator invokes moments of genocide and annihilation, with references to "eugenics" and "mushroom clouds" to describe the experience of being at home in the town. The overblown melding of the twee with an allusion to nuclear horror — "prettiest, freshest mushroom clouds" — is disquieting. Saturation, contamination, and death are presented as inherent to the scene. Fictional Boulder is a dead zone, teeming with decay and haunted by nightmares. Mike Kitchell describes the book as a "horror novel, but the only thing that's terrifying is the Boulder of Middle America."[21] The purity of the community, as in Galton's utopian fantasy, is safeguarded by violent death.

---

19 Ibid., 21.

20 Ibid., 5.

21 Mike Kitchell, "25 Points approaching *The Memoirs of JonBenet by Kathy Acker* by Michael Du Plessis," *HTMLGIANT,* http://htmlgiant.com/reviews/25-points-approaching-the-memoirs-of-jonbenet-by-kathy-acker-by-michael-du-plessis/.

2. Psychoanalysis

Luminol theory draws on psychoanalytic theory, amalgamating aspects of abject analysis (particularly the work of Julia Kristeva), queer theory (by reading with Judith Butler and against Lee Edelman and Leo Bersani), and the broad field of death studies (incorporating Freudian psychoanalysis, trauma theory, and necrophilia) to produce a radical textual reading strategy.

Julia Kristeva published her influential psychoanalytical essay on abject analysis, *Powers of Horror,* in 1980.[22] Kristeva is a feminist philosopher and psychoanalyst. Her work on the abject was derived through engagement with Jacques Lacan's work, more specifically by addressing the lack of the maternal figure in Lacan's formulation of the (motherless) mirror stage of infant subjective development.[23] In Kristeva's reading, the abject refers to a state that is neither (o)bject nor (sub)ject but (a)bject. Outside, beyond, and cast out of the symbolic order, "the jettisoned object [...] is radically excluded and draws me toward the place where meaning collapses."[24] According to Kristeva, the most acute example of the abject is the cadaver, that which shows "what I permanently thrust aside in order to live" and illuminates the horror of "existing at the border of my condition as a living being."[25] Using abject analysis, Kristeva reads several examples of European literature in *Powers of Horror.* She is especially influenced by Céline, whose novel *L'Ecole des cadavres* explicitly references the corpse.[26]

Kristeva's notion of the abject has in turn been taken up by artists, literary theorists, and feminist scholars of horror. In fact,

22 Julia Kristeva, *Powers of Horror: An Essay on Abjection,* trans. Leon S. Roudiez (New York: Columbia University Press, 1982).

23 Jacques Lacan, "The Mirror-Phase as Formative of the Function of the I," *New Left Review,* no. 51 (1968): 71–77.

24 Kristeva, Powers of Horror, 2.

25 Ibid., 3.

26 Louis-Ferdinand Céline, *L'Ecole des cadavres* (Paris: Denoël, 1938). Kristeva is also influenced by James Joyce, Fyodor Dostoyevsky, the Comte de Lautréamont, Marcel Proust, Antonin Artaud, and Franz Kafka.

one of the most famous usages of Kristeva's abject is in Barbara Creed's reading of the film *Alien* (dir. Ridley Scott, 1979) and Creed's theory of the "monstrous feminine."[27] This highly influential version of the abject is "edged with the sublime"; it not only is cast out of the symbolic order but is also *sub* (askance, beneath, below) the limen between real and imaginary, self and other.[28] The abject is always liminal; it limns; it is sublime; it is inherent to luminol theory.

Judith Butler, a philosopher, feminist, and queer theorist, responded to Kristeva's formulation of the abject in a chapter of her book *Bodies That Matter* titled "Phantasmatic Identification and the Assumption of Sex."[29] Published almost a decade after *Powers of Horror, Bodies That Matter* was Butler's follow-up to her seminal work of queer theory, *Gender Trouble.*[30] Although *Bodies That Matter* was in some ways an attempt to clarify the arguments of the first book, it was also Butler's contribution to an ongoing discourse of queer theory and gender studies. In this latter capacity, Butler appraised *Powers of Horror* and identified the heteronormative nature of the abject maternal in Kristeva's formulation.

Luminol theory binds Kristeva to Butler to produce what I call a "pro-abject" position: a position of erotic centrality for that which is cast out of the symbolic order. The pro-abject can be used in several ways. The first and most obvious way is to queer the heteronormative binaries that appear in post-Freudian psychoanalytic theory that foregrounds the nuclear family. A second way that the pro-abject can be deployed is as a redemptive tool, a means of reclaiming that which has been cast out. Leo Bersani, a literary theorist and psychoanalytic scholar, argues in his book *The Culture of Redemption* (1990) that the

---

27 Barbara Creed, *The Monstrous-Feminine: Film, Feminism, Psychoanalysis* (London: Routledge, 1993).

28 Kristeva, *Powers of Horror*, 11.

29 Judith Butler, *Bodies That Matter: On the Discursive Limits of Sex* (1993; New York: Routledge, 2011).

30 Judith Butler, *Gender Trouble: Feminism and the Subversion of Identity*, 2nd ed. (1990; New York: Routledge, 2006).

overwhelming project of art, literature, and culture is to offer a means of comfort and redemption when set against the horror of reality.[31] He traces this collective act of narcissism through Sigmund Freud's work on sublimation and the psychoanalysis of culture. For Bersani, redemption is an illusory, sybaritic pleasure. The pro-abject is a means of reclaiming the redemptive in order to recenter the erotic by producing a redemptive necrophilia — that is, by prioritizing the most potent symbol of the abject, the cadaver, and engaging in an erotic discourse with the corpse as queering death itself. This strategy is partially taken up by Lacanian queer theorist Lee Edelman.

Edelman's *No Future: Queer Theory and the Death Drive,* published in 2004, argues for a radical politics of queering death.[32] Edelman's influential work argues that rather than looking to a hetero-procreative futurity, queerness should align itself with the death drive precisely because this disrupts and subverts heterogeneous and dominant ideological norms. Edelman's work could be considered a polemic, a queer call to arms in the face of increasingly assimilationist and heteronormative strategies for securing LGBTQ+ rights. Edelman's work binds queer theory to death studies to produce a deliberate aporia. In contrast, the pro-abject argues for a radical futurity of the death drive, a redemptive necrophilia.

Edelman works with a conception of the death drive originally formulated by Freud in his essay "Beyond the Pleasure Principle" (1920).[33] Freud's concept was at once radical and simple: that the goal of each living organism is to revert to the inorganic and to move toward death. This formulation has been taken up widely in psychoanalytic theory, trauma theory, and death studies. Cathy Caruth's work on trauma, profoundly informed by "Beyond the Pleasure Principle," provides a model

---

31 Leo Bersani, *The Culture of Redemption* (Cambridge: Harvard University Press, 1990).

32 Lee Edelman, No Future: Queer Theory and the Death Drive (Durham: Duke University Press, 2004).

33 Sigmund Freud, *Beyond the Pleasure Principle and Other Writings* (London: Penguin, 2003).

for the operation of luminol theory as a series of "flashbacks"[34] or fragments of light. Trauma scholars including Ruth Leys[35], Roger Luckhurst[36], and Shoshana Felman[37] have responded to and complicated Caruth's work in relation to Freud.

Lisa Downing, a psychoanalytic scholar who explores death studies, draws together the pro-abject, the queer, and the death drive as she argues for a broader cultural interpretation of necrophilia that goes beyond the pathology of the individual.[38] Finally, Elisabeth Bronfen's *Over Her Dead Body* provides a cultural history of the dead girl in cultural representation and argues for a close relationship between death, the feminine, and the aesthetic.[39]

The three main theoretical strands of luminol theory — abject analysis, queer theory, and death studies — are inextricably linked, as demonstrated by this brief outline of key theorists and theories. Luminol theory brings each of these aspects together in order to produce a textual reading strategy that excavates narrative just as luminol excavates the crime scene.

---

34 Cathy Caruth, *Unclaimed Experience* (Baltimore: John Hopkins Press, 1996), 65.

35 Ruth Leys, *Trauma: A Genealogy* (Chicago: University of Chicago Press, 2000).

36 Roger Luckhurst, *The Trauma Question* (London and New York: Routledge, 2013).

37 Shoshana Felman, *Testimony: Crises of Witnessing in Literature, Psychoanalysis, History* (London and New York: Routledge, 1992).

38 Lisa Downing, *Desiring the Dead: Necrophilia and Nineteenth-Century French Literature* (Oxford: Legenda, 2003).

39 Elisabeth Bronfen, *Over Her Dead Body: Death, Femininity and the Aesthetic* (Manchester: Manchester University Press, 1992).

3. Hermeneutics

Hermeneutic excavation is a form of depth reading, an analytical process that seeks to uncover subtextual, or otherwise buried, meaning below the surface of the text. It is aligned with Paul Ricœur's "hermeneutics of suspicion" and with Michel Foucault's interrelated concepts of archaeology and genealogy. Luminol theory can be understood as a version of depth reading that has many points of congruence with existing methods. The forensic aspect of luminol theory aligns it with Ricœur's use of suspicion from the lexicon of the police detective; the excavatory function aligns it with Foucault's archaeological theory.

Foucault developed his related concepts of archaeology and genealogy in his essay "Nietzsche, Genealogy, History" and his book *The Archaeology of Knowledge*.[40] In the latter, Foucault outlines his archaeological metaphor as it pertains to the reading of historical and cultural artifacts:

The tools that enable historians to carry out this work of analysis are partly inherited and partly of their own making: models of economic growth, quantitative analysis of market movements, accounts of demographic expansion and contraction, the study of climate and its long-term changes, the fixing of sociological constants, the description of technological adjustments and of their spread and continuity. These tools have enabled workers in the historical field to distinguish various sedimentary strata; linear successions, which for so long had been the object of research, have given way to discoveries in depth. From the political mobility at the surface down to the slow movements of "material civilisation," ever more levels of analysis have been established: each has

---

40 Michel Foucault, "Nietzsche, Genealogy, History," in *Language, Counter-Memory, Practice: Selected Essays and Interviews,* ed. Donald F. Bouchard (Ithaca: Cornell University Press, 1980), 139–64; Michel Foucault, *The Archaeology of Knowledge,* trans. A.M. Sheridan Smith (1972; London: Routledge, 2002).

> its own peculiar discontinuities and patterns; and as one de-
> scends to the deepest levels, the rhythms become broader.[41]

Foucault here articulates a complex set of ideas: that the tools a historian uses are always in flux; that these tools can be both pre-existing and improvised, both macro and micro; that history is unstable and deep, with 'sediments' and 'strata,' rather than linear, chronological, and progressive. Perhaps most pertinent to this book, is the idea that the deeper the archaeologist excavates, the more chaotic and unstable the notion of history becomes and the more subject it is to "peculiar discontinuities and patterns." Further, Foucault elaborates the unit in which history is measured out: the document. According to him, "history is the work expanded on material documentation (books, texts accounts, registers, acts, buildings, institutions, laws, techniques, objects, customs, etc.)."[42] He claims that in "its traditional form" history "undertook to 'memorise' the monuments of the past," that is, to reify historical experience in a specific, memorializing way. But the archaeological thought, he argues, allows history to be understood as functioning in the opposite manner, "transform[ing] *documents* into *monuments*." Once Foucault has outlined the field on which the archaeologist works, he goes on to define his concept more precisely as a tool to cut to the bone of the artefacts it reads, defining "discourses themselves, those discourses as practices obeying certain rules" rather than seeking "another better-hidden discourse"; as "quite alien" to the "principle of unity" of the oeuvre; and "not a return to the innermost secret of the origin" but the "systematic description of the discourse-object."[43]

For Foucault, genealogy is closely related to the archaeological method. He describes genealogy as "grey, meticulous, and patiently documentary. It operates on a field of entangled and

---

41 Foucault, *Archaeology of Knowledge,* 3.
42 Foucault also describes history as turning away from "vast unities like 'periods' or 'centuries' to the phenomena of rupture, of discontinuity." Ibid., 6.
43 Ibid., 155–56.

confused parchments, on documents that have been scratched over and recopied many times."[44] This describes a palimpsestic text, a text that can be excavated or "scratched" through for meaning. Yet these palimpsestic texts are tangled; it is impossible to find out which one is the ur-text. Rather than pursuing the essentialist mode of attempting to "capture the exact essence of things, their purest possibilities, and their carefully protected identities," if the genealogist "listens to history" they may find "that there is "something altogether different" below the surface: not a timeless and essential secret, but the secret that they have no essence or that their essence was fabricated in a piecemeal fashion from alien forms.[45] This way of understanding history is deeply disturbing, as it shifts the bedrock of history from a linear, chronological narrative to one that is arbitrary and senseless.[46]

---

44 Foucault, "Nietzsche, Genealogy, History," 139.

45 Ibid., 141.

46 In fact, Foucault acknowledges this, saying of those who oppose his methods: "At all costs, they must preserve that tiny fragment of discourse — whether written or spoken — whose fragile, uncertain existence must perpetuate their lives. They cannot bear (and one cannot but sympathise) to hear someone saying: 'Discourse is not life: its time is not your time; in it, you will not be reconciled to death; you may have killed God beneath the weight of all that you have said; but don't imagine that, with all that you are saying, you will make a man that will live longer than he.'" Foucault, *Archaeology of Knowledge*, 211. His unsettled approach to history was highly influential to Ruth Leys in her work *Trauma: A Genealogy*. Leys argues that she takes a "genealogical approach to the study of trauma, in an effort to understand what Michel Foucault has called 'the singularity of events outside any monotonous finality' and in order to register their recurrence, as he has put it, not for the purpose of tracing 'the gradual curve of their evolution, but to isolate the different scenes where they engaged in different roles.'" Ruth Leys, *Trauma: A Genealogy* (Chicago: University of Chicago Press, 2000), 8. Murray M. Schwartz, reviewing *Trauma: A Genealogy*, reflects on the specifically deconstructionist way that Leys uses genealogy: "The organic concept of genealogy describes unities that unfold in time. There is no unity to be found, however, in the conflicting and often incompatible assumptions of trauma theories as Leys investigates them. She deals with the ways in which trauma theories have repeatedly led to unresolved problems, impasses, or — in the vocabulary of deconstruction — aporias."

This deeply unsettling, "alien" form of history is the key to Ricœur's "hermeneutics of suspicion," an influential depth-reading strategy "inextricably involved with the recovery of meaning."[47] Ricoeur's first clear published analysis of the term "the hermeneutics of suspicion" appears in the foreword to Don Ihde's book, *Hermeneutic Phenomenology: The Philosophy of Paul Ricœur* (1971), has a foreword by Ricœur that contains his first clear and published analysis of the term "the hermeneutics of suspicion."[48] According to Alison Scott-Baumann, Ricœur "uses the term hermeneutics of suspicion to refer to Freud and Hegel, to the 'hidden depth meaning of a text which the *hermeneutics of suspicion* allow to emerge' and to the dialectical opposition between the hermeneutics of suspicion and phenomenology."[49] In the same preface, Ricœur makes specific reference to archaeology when he discusses how Freud develops a detour backwards, an archaeological dig into the unconscious mind of the child inside the adult.[50]

In *Freud and Philosophy: An Essay on Interpretation* (1970) Ricœur shows how Freud's model of interpretation was particularly suited to symbolic language, which Ricoeur defined as any form of language "where another meaning is both given and hidden in an immediate meaning."[51] Ricœur posited that the symbolic function was "to mean something other than what is said,"[52] and posited that "to interpret is to understand a double meaning."[53] What he called a "hermeneutics of suspicion" in Freud described a method of understanding double mean-

Murray M. Schwartz, "Locating Trauma: A Commentary on Ruth Leys's Trauma: A Genealogy," *American Imago* 59, no. 3 (2002): 369.

47 Alison Scott-Baumann, *Ricœur and the Hermeneutics of Suspicion* (London: Continuum, 2009), 63.

48 Don Ihde, foreword to Paul Ricœur, *Hermeneutic Phenomenology: The Philosophy of Paul Ricœur* (Evanston: Northwestern University Press, 1971).

49 Scott-Baumann, *Ricœur and the Hermeneutics of Suspicion,* 63.

50 Don Ihde, foreword to Ricœur, *Hermeneutic Phenomenology.*

51 Paul Ricœur, *Freud and Philosophy,* trans. Denis Savage (New Haven: Yale University Press, 1970), 7.

52 Ibid.

53 Ibid., 8.

ing based not on the religious model of revealed meaning but on the demystification of illusion.[54] This secular reading of the "double meaning" rejects the idea of a fixed, revealed truth that lies behind the explicit content of a text. In Ricœur's system, a suspicious reading instead posits "a kind of mourning of the immediate."[55] This kind of reading has application in luminol theory because it both reveals the instability of meaning and acts in a compassionate, memorializing way.

A marriage of Foucault and Ricœur can be seen in D.A. Miller's *The Novel and the Police*. Miller argues that the novel itself is "the story of an active regulation" — part of a closed system with other regulatory state apparatuses, both ideological and repressive.[56] Using Foucauldian logic, Miller enacts something like Ricœur's hermeneutics of suspicion upon the realist novel, specifically the nineteenth-century realist novel. By reading *Oliver Twist,* for example, as a carceral world where the "happy family" that Oliver is temporarily fostered into is simply another regulatory institution — like the workhouse, the orphanage, or the prison, it exerts discipline and temporal control over the individual — Miller exposes that "after all what brought carceral institutions into being in the first place were lapses in the proper management of the family." Baby farms, orphanages, debtors prisons, and workhouses were created in response to illegitimate children, poverty, and debt.[57] He also argues that the portrayal of a different kind of policing by a paranoid, secret police in the realist novel of this era marks a move from "spectacular punishment to a hidden and devious discipline."[58] In other words, the rise of the realist novel, contemporaneous with this

54 Stephen Best and Sharon Marcus, "Surface Reading: An Introduction," in *The Way We Read Now,* eds. Sharon Marcus and Stephen Best with Emily Apter and Elaine Freedgood, special issue, *Representations* 108, no. 1 (2009): 11.

55 Charles E. Reagan, *Paul Ricœur: His Life and His Work* (Chicago: University of Chicago Press, 1996), 100.

56 Miller, *The Novel and the Police,* 10.

57 Ibid., 59.

58 Ibid., 22.

shift to "a police defined in terms of the spatial extension of its networks and the temporal deployment of its intrigues" meant that "not unlike the novel, the new police has "charge of a 'world' and a 'plot.'"[59] Hence Miller encompasses both the novel and the police in a closed carceral system.

This type of suspicious reading, inherently to do with latent rather than manifest content, is the subject of an article by Stephen Best and Sharon Marcus where they argue for surface reading, or, as Marcus describes it, "just reading."[60] In Marcus's earlier book, *Between Women,* she acknowledges a debt to Foucault by titling a chapter "The Genealogy of Marriage," and, in "Just Reading," Best and Marcus explicitly describe themselves as heirs of "Michel Foucault, skeptical about the very possibility of radical freedom and dubious that literature or its criticism can explain our oppression or provide the keys to our liberation."[61] However, both writers believe that Foucault is missing an important possibility of literary criticism, that of attention to the surface as well as the depth. Marcus describes "just reading" in opposition to what is known as "symptomatic reading," with its overtones of pathology and illness. Marcus suggests:

> In the place of symptomatic readings, the interpretations I offer in this chapter are what I call "just readings." Just reading attends to what [Fredric] Jameson, in his pursuit

59 Ibid., 23.

60 Sharon Marcus, *Between Women: Friendship, Desire, and Marriage in Victorian England* (Princeton: Princeton University Press, 2007), 73–108. For more on the origins and applications of this approach, see Peter Brooks, *Reading for the Plot: Design and Intention in Narrative* (Cambridge: Harvard University Press, 1992); Regenia Gagnier, *Subjectivities: A History of Self-Representation in Britain, 1832–1920* (New York: Oxford University Press, 1991); D.A. Miller, *Narrative and Its Discontents: Problems of Closure in the Traditional Novel* (Princeton: Princeton University Press, 1981); Sandra M. Gilbert and Susan Gubar, *The Madwoman in the Attic: The Woman Writer and the Nineteenth-Century Literary Imagination,* 2nd ed. (New Haven: Yale University Press, 2000); and Rachel Blau DuPlessis, *Writing beyond the Ending: Narrative Strategies of Twentieth-Century Women Writers* (Bloomington: Indiana University Press, 1985).

61 Best and Marcus, "Surface Reading: An Introduction," 2.

of hidden master codes, dismisses as "the inert givens and materials of a particular text." In tracing the representation of female friendship in the Victorian novel, I do not claim to plumb hidden depths but to account more fully for what texts present on their surface but critics have failed to notice. I invoke the word "just" in its many senses. Just reading strives to be adequate to a text conceived as complex and ample rather than diminished by, or reduced to, what it has had to repress.[62]

"Just reading" is a specific version of surface reading that attends to the justness or fairness of reading what is on the page and not creating a false binary between latent and manifest content. Marcus suggests that depth reading has failed in the past not only by producing this binary, but also by failing to notice what is visible in the paranoid urge to discover what has been occulted.

Luminol theory is a form of depth reading in the tradition of Foucault and Ricœur, with its emphasis on excavation, removing layers, and revealing the autochthonous horror at the scene of history. It also, however, takes some political and ethical cues from Best and Marcus, attending not only to the depths but also to the surface, reading the text as palimpsestic rather than binary. Luminol theory, too, is invested in the tradition of using detection as a mode of literary criticism.[63] Literary critics, theorists, and historians frequently use the criminal and legal lexicon as metaphors for their work. Examples of this specific

---

62 Marcus, *Between Women*, 75.

63 For more on this tradition, see L.C. Knights, *How Many Children Had Lady MacBeth? An Essay in the Theory and Practice of Shakespeare Criticism* (Cambridge: Gordon Fraser, Minority Press, 1933); James Franklin, *The Science of Conjecture: Evidence and Probability before Pascal* (Baltimore: Johns Hopkins University Press, 2001); Calvin Hoffman, *The Murder of the Man Who Was "Shakespeare"* (1955; New York: Grosset & Dunlap, 1960); Susan Stewart, *Crimes of Writing: Problems in the Containment of Representation* (Durham: Duke University Press, 1994); and William Twining, *Rethinking Evidence: Exploratory Essays* (Evanston: Northwestern University Press, 1990).

pairing of the language of detection and literary criticism can be found in Jack Lynch's book *Deception and Detection in Eighteenth-Century Britain,* which employs criminal, police, and legal language ("conviction," "evidence," "observation," "motive," "facts," "uniform") to interrogate eighteenth-century hoaxes.[64] This kind of detection is itself an adjunct of the centrality of the case study to psychoanalysis.[65] What luminol theory does differently from pre-existing forms of depth reading is to explicitly pair forensic procedures, specifically the application of luminol at the crime scene, with excavatory readings. It also offers a voice to the marginalized, to the dead at the scene, by approaching what is clearly the subject of the archaeological or suspicious reading — the discovered corpse — through the application of the forensic imaginary.

---

64 Jack Lynch, *Deception and Detection in Eighteenth-Century Britain* (Aldershot: Ashgate, 2008).

65 For more on this, see Henry Bond, *Lacan at the Scene* (Cambridge: MIT Press, 2009); Charles Bernheimer and Claire Kahane, eds., *In Dora's Case: Freud — Hysteria — Feminism,* 2nd ed. (New York: Columbia University Press, 1990); Sigmund Freud, *The "Wolfman" and Other Cases,* trans. Louise Adey Huish (London: Penguin Classics, 2002); Sigmund Freud, *Three Case Histories* (1963; New York: Touchstone, 2008).

At the luminol-drenched crime scene: flashes of illumination throw up words, sentences, and fragments that offer luminous, strange glimpses, bobbing up from below their polished surfaces.

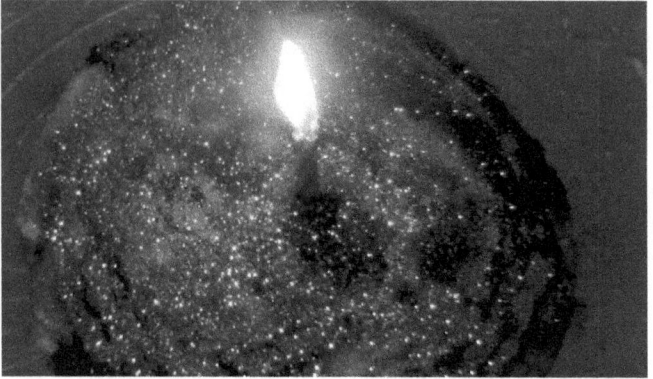

Figure 3. The Abject Parlor. Still from *The Luminol Reels*.

The Abject Parlor
Polyester Gothic, Traces at the Crime Scene, Christmas in Colorado

Elements drawn from the familiar appear to be blurring and combining, their ordinary domestic contexts jettisoned. A packet of Coleman's Instant Mashed Potato can be seen next to some worn lady's stockings. Next to this is a large piece of polythene and other textile garments, with what looks like underwear discarded on a large pile of unprotected LP records (fragile objects, designed to be carefully returned to their sleeves), a torn book cover, a broken lampshade, fragments of crockery, a lone hair curler. A wider view of the scene — photograph 4.2 — reveals a saucepan inexplicably placed on a bedroom cabinet, waste receptacles overturned or unused. In photograph 4.3, a suitcase is depicted with a large hole [in] it — the contents accessed unconventionally.
— Henry Bond, *Lacan at the Scene*

1. Polyester Gothic

> *Will something that looks almost exactly human extract my brain*
> *stem, cloak me in polyester, and chain me to the gas barbecue?*
> — Kim Ian Michasiw, "Some Stations of Suburban Gothic"

Luminol theory uncovers what I am describing as Polyester Gothic, that is, the romantically bewitching contemporary narratives of trailer parks, motels, shopping malls, and tract housing — spaces where the cheap, decaying, toxic materials that make up the prefabricated dwellings, the polka-dot bikinis, and the disposable jewelry that litter the landscape of this genre are not incidental but central to the horror invoked. Each object becomes freighted with meaning, its surface in contact with human matter — matter that can be read with luminol.

As a study of Middle American banality as romance, *The Memoirs of JonBenét Ramsey by Kathy Acker* is a perfect example of Polyester Gothic. The snow-soiled, faded fabrics that crinkle through *Memoirs* represent the postindustrial decay of a pretty mountain town. In fact, Du Plessis is clearly still obsessed and romantically entangled with Boulder, and this break-up note is more of a renewal with that obsession than a clear escape. Because of this, he manages a tender, affectionate tone, even.

The fictional inhabitants of the fictionalized Boulder in *Memoirs* suffer a microcosmic imprisonment in a camp, tasteless object. The tract housing that the characters occupy within the snow globe is brutally conformist, ugly, and decaying; beige carpet spreads from the apartments out into the landscape; there is no escape from the banality of horror. The narrator elides the claustrophobia of the tract houses, with their windowless seclusion and dilapidated furnishings, with the overall conceit of the snow globe that covers the fictionalized Boulder. Landscape and home are blurred; the exterior and the interior have no real meaning for the narrator, JonBenét. No matter how many times she shape-shifts, no matter how powerful her knowledge or how witchy her resurrection, she is always stuck in this airless, tacky pod. The curiously adult voice proclaims, "I'm drowning in a vacuum, surrounded on all sides by the yards of gravel and bark that my neighbors consider landscaping."[1] The snow globe can be thought of as pre-existing the fictionalized Boulder, and at the same time being a disposable, cheap, and arbitrary object. Additionally, the snow globe, described explicitly as "bought in a cheap airport gift store," is part of the capitalist project, an item whose inception has caused several potential harms: sweatshop labor, environmental pollution, and economic oppression.[2] Before capitalism, this version of Boulder could not have existed and would not have made any sense. This object, a remnant of capitalism, would perhaps continue to exist even if capitalist structures became obsolete. The explicit reference to the "ugly" nature of the object means that it occupies the aesthetic domain and yet is found wanting. In *Memoirs,* the environmental is the plastic and the aesthetic is the political. This connection to assembly-line capitalist practices is not accidental; in fact, plastic is often aligned with the capitalist project, derived as it is from oil. The disposability of plastic is also an ecological concern and linked to fears around mortality through the specter of global warming.

It is not only the snow globe that is made of plastic; all of the private tastes and furnishings in the Boulder of *Memoirs* are composed of cheap plastic materials. The character of Kathy Acker in the book has a long soliloquy on the "unmitigated horror of the domestic space in Boulder." It is worth reproducing this passage in full:

Structures of the 1970s, they promised the good life of the American Bicentennial in the raw materials — particle board, polyresin, reinforced tupperware, drywall, polyester, pressed wood shingle, polyurethane — the flammable and cheap fabric on which the American Dream is spun. All apartments are alike: beige carpeting, grey from years of snow stains, pet stains, brown kitchen sticky from years of unsavory veg-

---

1   Du Plessis, *Memoirs,* 4.

2   Ibid., 3.

etarian grease, dank bathroom in dark green. Look, the A-frame with its two-storey wood-burning fireplace, cozy, no? A wood-burning stove in every A-frame, those kitchens in once-modish browns, those bathrooms of an avocado color trendy long ago: hippie dreams met money in a studio jam-session bliss-out, in a free-love encounter of leisure architec-ture and rising real-estate values. Olive green, brown, beige, camouflage colours still, after Vietnam, violently neutral, U.S. foreign policy turned domestic design.[3]

This speech argues that decisions about taste and furnishing that are made in private in Boulder have had a direct correlation with war, capitalism, and other violent crimes against human-ity. Du Plessis sees the structural inequalities of the American Dream as being tied directly to matters of domesticity. The av-ocado bathroom suite is interchangeable with the camouflage worn by soldiers in Vietnam. Truly these are crimes of taste.

This sinister banality is figured through the cheap raw ma-terials that build the uniform A-frame houses. Their lack of in-dividuality and lack of engagement with natural resources dis-plays a short-term toxic relationship with the environment and a lacuna of imagination that negates empathy with those who are different. The environment enacts brutal indifference. There is also a strong sense of fakeness, and a lack of authenticity that attaches to materials that are not considered natural: fiberboard, polyester, etc. These materials are designed to mimic those found in nature, such as wood, silk, and wool; yet they are non-biodegradable and potentially toxic. This fakeness is both physi-cal and political. Not only does the plastic matter in *Memoirs* damage the environment of Boulder, it also subdues radicalism and dissent. The Boulder of this novella is uncanny. It shows us the mundane and the homely, and then undercuts this coziness with shifting perspectives, characters who fluctuate, and a death that recurs over and over; a human sacrifice on an epic scale. Boulder is also an abject zone and there is a psychopathic drive

---

3   Ibid., 22–23.

to murder JonBenét to sacrifice her in order to generate tourism and interest, or, in a term coined by writer and critic Johannes Göransson, *atrocity kitsch*.[4]

Göransson coined the term atrocity kitsch to describe the interconnectedness of the kitsch and the tacky with atrocities of all descriptions.[5] Göransson uses "atrocity kitsch" to describe work by a variety of artists, filmmakers, and writers, primarily poets, whose work centers sacred, contaminated artifacts. As well as established artists such as David Lynch and Sylvia Plath, the concept includes Charles Manson and the Abu Ghraib photographs. Göransson's own work, the obscenely unperformable *Entrance to a Colonial Pageant in Which We All Began to Intricate,* is explicitly positioned as an example of atrocity kitsch; one of the characters, Mimesis, says directly to the audience: "I want to be your atrocity kitsch."[6] So is Olivia Cronk's *Skin Horse,* a book-length poem that Action Books, the radical press run by Göransson and his partner, poet and scholar Joyelle McSweeney, published in 2012.[7] When I asked McSweeney via email why they decided to publish *Skin Horse,* she replied, "I would say the uncanny power in this book comes from its peaks and declivities, its fragmentation which ends up hosting an infernal and illimitable pow'r."[8] This description references both the supernatural, occult aspect of the poem, and also the palimpsestic, contaminative function of the text as it "hosts": it is a crime scene, burial ground, or horror film. Cronk explicitly links *Skin Horse* to the cinematic, arguing that "poetry and film are siblings." She also contends that in film "(1) the images (text(s)) can bleed into/leak onto/become others and one another; and (2) the medium

---

4   This term was first discussed by Göransson in the following blog entry: Johannes Göransson, "Atrocity Kitsch," *Montevidayo* (blog), August 18, 2010, http://www.montevidayo.com/atrocity-kitsch/.

5   Ibid.

6   Johannes Göransson, *Entrance to a Colonial Pageant in Which We All Begin to Intricate* (Grafton: Tarpaulin Sky Press, 2011), 71.

7   Olivia Cronk, *Skin Horse* (Notre Dame: Action Books, 2012). *Skin Horse*'s pages are unnumbered.

8   Joyelle McSweeney, email exchange with author, January 2015.

itself, especially given the current iterations via YouTube, phone culture, etc., transmits and explodes."[9] In *Skin Horse* the mode of writing itself can "transmit," "leak," and "bleed," contaminating and infecting culture.

For Göransson, Americana, ephemera, and junk do not conceal atrocities, but rather are the means by which atrocities function. In *Skin Horse,* this means that the most heinous moments of sadistic violence can be enacted through kitschy objects like lipstick, ketchup, and crystal balls. *Skin Horse* converts ephemera into aesthetic material. The poem also pays special attention to those artifacts that have some relationship with futurity and natural cycles. Fakeness, plasticity, toxicity, and metamorphosis are all important concepts in *Skin Horse.*

Skin Horse does not distinguish between the natural landscape and man-made artifacts, as evidenced by lines such as "The pond was a bad window" and "The place is polyester."[10] There is an apparent privileging in *Skin Horse* of throwaway objects; items such as lipstick, blisters, flyers, and ketchup take on occult and sacred resonances. The objects in Cronk's work bring theoretical pressure to bear on the text. In this way they can be closely aligned with the hyperobjects of Timothy Morton's formulation, that is, they are objects that do not conform in any way to linear or spatial regularity; they are objects that are *beyond.*[11]

Skin Horse does something complex and strange with its ephemera. Not only does the poem refuse to distinguish between separate categories of the plastic and the static and the authentic and the fake, it also insists on a specific kind of futurity — one that relies on the melding of the banal and the sacred in lines such as "a crystal ball flyer in my bag" and "What lipstick lights. / Through a branch, one creeped to scream."[12] The crystal ball flyer is the perfect example of the sacred throwaway

9   Olivia Cronk, email exchange with author, September 2014.
10 Cronk, *Skin Horse.*
11 Timothy Morton, *The Ecological Thought* (Cambridge: Harvard University Press, 2012).
12 Cronk, *Skin Horse.*

object. Both the flyer and the crystal ball it represents are plastic objects: the flyer is made from cheap, toxic materials and the crystal ball, though glass, is a symbol of the plasticity of future and present. The weight accorded to the occult potential of the crystal ball is undercut by the tackiness and commerciality of the flyer. The "lipstick lights" that call to mind a cosmetic artificiality are also, somehow, luminous. This image of bright, glowing colors illuminating a part of the forest where one "creeped to scream" is unsettling; the childlike innocence of the lipstick is displaced by the potential site of violence and trauma invoked by the scream. This tension is present throughout the poem, and the theme of violence to children is repeated in the line:

a concrete head rises doomily from a parking lot
to watch children come falling in their own awful ketchup.[13]

This line is, again, a melding of the banal and the numinous, the natural and the synthetic. "Ketchup" is a widely understood signifier for fake blood and calls to mind both the ultimate Americana of low-budget slasher films and Halloween costumes, as well as junk food and diners. To have the children "falling in their own awful ketchup" hints at a sadistic desire to enact violence and perhaps even murder. Though this desire is focalized through the "concrete head" rising "doomily" from a "parking lot," which on first read could be considered a detached, potentially absurd point of view, there is an alignment between the man-made concrete and the man-made ketchup. The line invokes an entire world of human endeavor: it is not nature that is to be feared, but the humans who watch impassively as children continue to suffer violence from man-made causes. There are other places in the poem where death is presented as a Freudian nightmare:

My morbid, awful dying in clean boots.
Nostalgia

---

13   Ibid.

for teeth clattering out[14]

This death is so horrific that the loss of teeth, a hyper-Freudian symbol of humiliation, is considered nostalgic. This death is more "morbid," more "awful": an utterly humiliating death that does not respect clean boots or any other human strategy to combat fear through control and order.

There are several instances in *Skin Horse* of the natural world functioning as a technological space or museum. The narrator writes near the beginning of the poem that they "came to cringe at the miniature eggs," then announces shortly afterwards, "I heard of the trees typewritering." In these statements there is a sense that a human entity is dominating the landscape of *Skin Horse* and applying cultural content to it. The museum-like appropriation of the "miniature eggs" has an echo of Carl Fabergé's decadent creations for the Romanov imperial family, while the "typewritering" trees present an uncanny image of automatic writing, the fusion of the natural and the technological.[15] Other examples of artificial matter include gloves, an ashtray that "spills on and on the edge of a pink seat," and nylons, a quaint term for hosiery that reminds the reader of war shortages and American soldiers and is a clear example of Cronk's invocation of Americana.[16] These everyday objects take on a plastic significance. The ashtray is a repository for waste, and the mingling

---

14 Ibid.

15 Of Fabergé's eggs, Toby Faber writes: "Whether fairly or not, their opulence and occasional vulgarity mean that they have come to symbolize the decadence of the court for which they were made. 'Now I understand why they had a revolution' is the common remark of someone viewing these creations for the first time. They may be masterpieces, but they also embody extravagance that even the Romanovs' most ardent supporter would find hard to justify. After 1917's inevitable cataclysm, the eggs disappeared in the chaos of the times." The "opulence and occasional vulgarity" to which Faber refers is foregrounded in a March 2006 story he cites about supermodel Kate Moss, who "smuggled the drugs Ecstasy and Rohypnol in a £65,000 gem-encrusted Faberge egg — clearly a replica." Toby Faber, *Faberge's Eggs: One Man's Masterpieces and the End of an Empire* (London: Pan, 2009), 4, 3.

16 Cronk, *Skin Horse.*

of the ash with the "pink seat" suggests an uneasy disruption of categories. The used, carcinogenic ash despoils the homely pink seat. The gloves become "enchanted" and "The place is polyester." Cheap, everyday materials take on transcendent properties in the world of *Skin Horse*. This transcendence can also take on a strong erotic charge when artificial objects are put to sadomasochistic use: "the dress-shoe blister gone wet"; "This pleather strap"; and

> On a lap I dress for dinner.
> I see to my old man's tongue
> caught on a tooth
> just as the word tunnel
> finishes.
> I smack it out on a leather wall. [17]

The "dress shoe" and the "pleather strap" are both related to notorious elements of fetishism: high-heeled shoes and spankings. The pinching of the dress shoe, causing blisters, indicates physical pain associated with the foot: a congruence of masochism and fetishism at a single site. That the blister has "gone wet" has overt sexual connotations. The pleather strap, made of a plastic, artificial material that replicates the cruelty of animal leather, is discussed in relation to "lap," "tooth," and "tongue" and has clear sexual overtones. The final line in this stanza, "I smack it out on a leather wall," commingles the natural and the artificial and describes an act of onomatopoeic violence that brings the reader back to the image of the strap.

The fetishized element becomes abject: it is partialized, synecdochic, and cast out of a symbiotic wholeness. Yet it also regulates sexual practices and confines them to specific strictures. Kristeva's formulation of the abject could be described as regulatory. By understanding the abject as that which is "cast out of the symbolic order," she defines what the symbolic order is. Hal Foster asks whether the abject, rather than being "disrup-

---

17   Ibid.

tive of subjective and social orders," could be "somehow foun-
dational of them."[18] This reading of the abject suggests that the
exclusion of "the alien within" turns abjection into a regulatory
operation.[19] Cronk, however, does not perform abjection in such
a definitive manner. She does not use abjection to regulate, but
rather to reveal, in the tradition of apocalyptic texts. The natural
world in *Skin Horse* is a disaster zone. The characters, and by im-
plication the reader, are "stepping on a million glass roaches."[20]
They "die and rush into the planet."[21] Animals, humans, and objects are interchangeable elements of atrocity kitsch. In this in-
terconnected, multivalent universe there is no radical exclusion.

Objects in *Skin Horse* are often plastic, man-made, and artificial and yet interact with sublime planes such as weather, sea-
sons, and landscape. *Skin Horse* imbues its objects with a nonlin-
ear relationship with time in a way that is similar to the futurity
outlined in Timothy Morton's *The Ecological Thought,* when our
descendants' "treatment of hyperobjects may seem like rever-
ence to our eyes."[22] In *Skin Horse,* the horror is even more tem-
porally acute where the apocalypse is perpetually in the present.
In this way, the Book of Revelation is a clear intertext for *Skin
Horse.* The perpetrator of evil in Revelation is a nebulous, mul-
tifaceted presence, but perhaps the most infamous incarnation
of evil in the book is the Whore of Babylon. She is introduced
in chapter 17, and the description is rich and poetic, though utterly misogynistic: "And the woman was arrayed in purple and
scarlet color, and decked with gold and precious stones and
pearls, having a golden cup in her hand full of abominations
and filthiness of her fornication."[23] This scene is excessive — she
is wearing purple, scarlet, and gold, and she is decked with "precious stones and pearls." These excesses signal a lack of modesty;

18 Hal Foster, *The Return of the Real: The Avant-Garde at the End of the Cen-
    tury* (Cambridge: MIT Press, 1996), 114.

19 Ibid., 115.

20 Cronk, *Skin Horse.*

21 Ibid.

22 Morton, *The Ecological Thought,* 132.

23 Revelation 17:4.

in fact, we are then told that the cup she is holding is "full of abominations and filthiness of her fornication."[24] There could be no clearer sign that aesthetic indulgence is directly linked to sexual impropriety. As the Whore of Babylon is invoked in Revelation as a warning sign of the coming apocalypse, there is a clear indication that women who attain economic and sexual freedom are imagined as frightening and dangerous. Cronk reverses this misogynistic omen by creating a set of revelations of her own and transmuting the high drama of Revelation into a work of atrocity kitsch. Where the Whore of Babylon has a golden cup filled with abominations, the narrator of *Skin Horse* says, "I know that   can see the strings of glue where the stone was joined to the cheap gold crown and its chain."[25] By seeing how cheap and man-made the gold crown is, by understanding the constructed nature of this kitsch item, Cronk draws attention to the constructedness of the patriarchal, feudal power systems that the crown represents.

Later in the poem Cronk writes of an analogous item to the golden cup filled with abominations, but in *Skin Horse,* the vessel is a gym bag:

> and they found a gym bag and opened it and in it found
> many terrible things and it was autumn and wheaty and
>   blue and in it many
> terrible things, the unzipping, the terrible unzipping noise
>   while we were
> combing[26]

The gym bag mentioned in this passage functions in a similar way to the golden cup of Revelation in that it is a vessel for numinous, unknowable horror. However, this item is a cheap, throwaway, and mass-manufactured plastic object. There is a

---

24 Ibid.

25 Cronk, *Skin Horse.* I have replicated the large spaces used by Cronk in the poem here.

26 Ibid.

narrative weight to the image of the gym bag as it is an item that can easily be imagined as an element of a crime or horror story, where typically it would be full of cash, guns, or drugs. The confusion between concrete and abstract here (i.e., the bag is purported to contain "autumn") echoes the earlier use of the golden cup to contain "fornication." The gym bag can therefore be read as the atrocity-kitsch version of the Whore of Babylon's golden cup.

2. Traces at the Crime Scene

> *Always arriving too late, the forensic photographer must depict instead only what is residual.*
> — Henry Bond, *Lacan at the Scene*

The opening of Toni Morrison's *The Bluest Eye* warps a familiar school textbook, the *Dick and Jane* reader series, in order to call attention to a sinister hidden narrative beneath the façade of the nuclear family. The first few pages reproduce a familiar passage three times, changing the layout each time. The first passage is reproduced accurately. It begins:

Here is the house. It is green and white. It has a red door. It is very pretty. Here is the family. Mother, Father, Dick, and Jane live in the green-and-white house. They are very happy.

The second time, Morrison removes the majority of the punctuation, which has the effect of disorienting the reader:

Here is the house it is green and white it has a red door it is very pretty here is the family mother father dick and jane live in the green-and-white house they are very happy

The third time, Morrison dispenses with all punctuation and all spacing. This creates a confusing jumble of words:

Hereisthehouseitisgreenandwhiteithasareddooritisveryprettyhereisthefamilymotherfatherdickandjaneliveinthegreenandwhitehousetheyareveryhappy[27]

The effect that Morrison creates is striking. By dismantling the ordered structure of the sentences, she calls attention to the chaos at the heart of the nuclear family.

---

27 Toni Morrison, *The Bluest Eye* (1970; London: Vintage, 1999), 1.

So too is the nuclear, Oedipal familial structure made strange in Cronk's poem; it is, in fact, made hyperabject. Cronk writes:

Husband your wife
is calling from the yard again
calling on
about those rat holes
in her peering deep[28]

Her language deliberately evokes a homely scene: husband, wife, yard, rat. On first view, this section of the poem reads almost as though it describes a household problem: a farm overrun with rats, or a wife not receiving support from her husband. What complicates and makes this poem strange are the more unusual language choices and word pairings she makes. When we hear that the wife is "calling on about those rat holes in her peering deep" there is an abject affect. The repetition of "calling" is frightening and suggests that the wife is calling out in distress. The "rat holes" suggest something rotting and decaying as well as fear of vermin and disease. And the wife's "peering deep" in conjunction with the "rat holes" calls to mind vaginal imagery. On closer inspection, this is an abject and alienating piece of writing that problematizes the Oedipal relationship and suggests a rottenness at the heart of family life. This is a hyperabject political strategy similar to the one Morrison employs in *The Bluest Eye*. Like Morrison, Cronk excavates a homely scene to reveal the hidden horror beneath. By foregrounding transgression and taboo, the hyperabject promotes what is unwholesome, rejected, and marginal and reveals the limitations of what is normative, traditional, and safe.

There is an abject erotics running through *Skin Horse* that centers the desire of subjects that would usually be "radically excluded"[29] or "jettisoned"[30] from erotic discourse. These sub-

---

28 Cronk, *Skin Horse.*
29 Kristeva, *Powers of Horror,* 2.
30 Ibid.

jects range from ones barely recognizable as human (corpses) to nonmammalian, alien life forms (lizards, squids). Near the beginning of the poem there is a highly sexualized, cultic moment that combines an erotics of death with polymorphous sexuality:

> watch
> your old friends
> the naked squids
> hung from a tree branch
> Screaming[31]

The figure of the squid can be read in two ways. An initial reading might place the scene generically within a horror narrative where "your … friends" are "screaming," "naked," and "hung from a tree branch." A second reading, however, which perceives the naked squid as polymorphous and multivalent, a creature that does not conform to a neat binary and is fleshly, inviting, and an object of desire. Much as Kristeva's description of the corpse can be seen as lexically aligned to desire and seduction so too the conjunction of "friends" with "naked," "screaming," and "hung" belong to the lexicon of sexual desire. This close relationship between sexual desire and death allows the radical possibilities of necrophilia as a form of alternative sexual strategy to be conceived. The following lines reinforce this dismantling of the heteronormative paradigm:

> Hanging the pond
> and reaching up to your utter
> metamorphosis.
>
> Lizard orgy.

---

31 Cronk, *Skin Horse.*

It unwifes me.
It unwifes me.
Unwifes me like a slid-in skin. Unwifes me. Unwifes me.[32]

Cronk's insistence here is on transcendent sexuality. The alien sexuality of the "lizard orgy" completes the "utter metamorphosis" of the addressee. The final repetition of "unwifes" is politically radical, breaking apart heteronormativity, female subservience, and the legal enforcement of patriarchal structures.

Cronk operates in the territory of the hyperabject; sexuality, gender, and desire are fluid in the poem. Not only is there radical potential for sexual experimentation with fetishism and sadomasochism, there is also ambiguity around the gender of the protagonist. Toward the end of the poem the narrator describes herself in this way: "There is someone very invisible standing inside of my body. And she is heating up, / boy is she."[33] These lines are spoken in a naïve voice, almost childlike in its simplicity. The conjunction of "boy" and "she" in the last line can be read as sexually ambiguous. Though "boy" can be interpreted here as a colloquialism, the commitment to polymorphous sexuality elsewhere in the poem — for example, in the section on squids near the beginning — indicates that this is a deliberate muddying of gendered pronouns. The sexual content of this line is heightened by the image of someone "inside" the narrator who is "heating up."

This heating can also be considered in the context of *Skin Horse* as an apocalyptic text in the tradition of Revelation. The ultimate hyperobject, according to Timothy Morton, is global warming.[34] As *Skin Horse* can be read as an apocalyptic text, the sexually charged "heating" in this extract can be read as hyperobject: first, it calls to mind the ur-hyperobject, global warming; second, it takes us into the realm of the abject, where boundaries of the body and of personhood are radically transgressed.

---

32 Ibid.
33 Ibid.
34 Morton, *The Ecological Thought*, 132.

In other places Cronk's work has more personal interactions with the dead and offers them care. There may be some more negative necrophiliac connotations in a line such as "comb the corpse's hair."[35] The power differential between the living being who is actively combing the corpse's hair is uncomfortable and calls to mind necrophilia. However, there is also a reading of this line that elucidates the care that the living person is giving to the corpse. This grooming practice can be considered as an inclusive or at the very least respectful form of interaction between the living and the dead. That the corpse is so seductive to the figure combing its hair would be unsurprising to Kristeva. In *Powers of Horror* she says, "The corpse, seen without God and outside of science, is the utmost of abjection. It is death infecting life. Abject. It is something rejected from which one does not part, from which one does not protect oneself as from an object. Imaginary uncanniness and real threat, it beckons to us and ends up engulfing us."[36] Though she describes a negative, threatening experience, the words she chooses could be interpreted as belonging to the lexicon of seduction, even love. The corpse is something "from which one does not part"; it "beckons" and ends up "engulfing" us. So too does the corpse in Cronk's poem behave seductively to the figure who is combing its hair, and by extension to the reader.

---

35 It is useful here to go back to Seamus Heaney's comments on the dual relationship that we have with the ancient burial of bodies: "Once upon a time, these heads and limbs existed in order to express and embody the needs and impulses of an individual human life. They were the vehicles of different biographies and they compelled singular attention, they proclaimed 'I am I.' Even when they were first dead, at the moment of sacrifice or atrocity, their bodies and their limbs manifested biography and conserved vestiges of personal identity: they were corpses. But when a corpse becomes a bog body, the personal identity drops away; the bog body does not proclaim 'I am I'; instead it says something like 'I am it' or 'I am you.' Like the work of art, the bog body asks to be contemplated; it eludes the biographical and enters the realm of the aesthetic." Seamus Heaney, "The Man and the Bog," in *Bog Bodies, Sacred Sites, and Wetland Archaeology,* eds. Bryony Coles, John Coles, and Mogens Schou Jørgensen (Exeter: Wetland Archaeology Research Project, 1999), 4.

36 Kristeva, *Powers of Horror,* 4.

The disgust that the living might ordinarily experience when confronted by the putrefaction of the dead is given an erotic and even ecstatic cast in *Skin Horse*. The poem deals with bodily fluids and scatology, showing an obsession with filth, decay, and organic ooze that is one of the main tenets of the abject as theorized by Kristeva: "Excrement and its equivalents (decay, infection, disease, corpse, etc.) stand for the danger to identity that comes from without: the ego threatened by the non-ego, society threatened by its outside, life by death."[37] Kristeva draws on earlier work by anthropologist Mary Douglas, whose book *Purity and Danger* provides an example of the hyperabject in operation in an anecdote about Catherine of Sienna: "St. Catherine of Sienna, when she felt revulsion from the wounds she was tending, is said to have bitterly reproached herself. Sound hygiene was incompatible with charity, so she deliberately drank of a bowl of pus."[38] Using luminol theory, I would argue that this contact with human waste to bring about a religious experience is a memorializing action, a closeness to death and disease that has a sacred aesthetic.

In *Skin Horse* blood and other organic human waste can be illuminated to reveal hidden narratives. Cronk writes:

> I went to see the dead men bleed
> But couldn't find the balcony.

And:

> My nose bled a velvet collar
> and growling a face dripped
> down into
> my bra.
> The room it fell to moody and livid pinings.[39]

---

37 Ibid., 71.
38 Mary Douglas, *Purity and Danger: An Analysis of the Concepts of Pollution and Taboo* (1966; London: Routledge, 2002), 7.
39 Cronk, *Skin Horse*.

This preoccupation with blood and bleeding is a hyperabject strategy. Cronk first makes the reader aware of the materiality of the blood that leaks from every orifice, every object, yet is in some indefinable way completely obscure. The voyeuristic desire to "see the dead men bleed" makes the reader complicit, as there is a sense of disappointment in the thwarted attempt when the protagonist is unable to "find the balcony." The balcony clearly signals a scopophilic space for spectacle, a theater of some kind. The lack of visual access frustrates the protagonist's, and the reader's, voyeuristic impulses. Cronk takes the scene into hyperabject territory, that is, territory where the abject is given centrality and reintegrated into the aesthetic, though it remains — as in Kristeva's famous formulation — cast out of the symbolic order. By the time the blood has begun to bleed "a velvet collar" and fall into the pattern of "moody and livid pinings" there has clearly been a transformation; the blood is both a trace reminder of violence and a force for progressive, artistic creation. This movement of blood from violent aporia to aesthetic design mirrors the function of luminol. Luminol not only reacts with blood to excavate and illuminate narratives that are otherwise frustratingly obscured (in the way the "dead men" are in this passage), it also creates art from horrific, brutal materials.

Skin Horse presents organic and inorganic materials as inherently connected. Dead animals, humans, and even planets interconnect, as do plastic objects. *Skin Horse* is written as one continuous poem with no numbered pages, and it is possible to dip in and out at any point. This combination of zoetrope — like endlessness and its shattered, fragmentary character offers a commentary on the nature of mortality, our mortality — our mortality as humans and the mortality of our planet. Though we cannot conceive of our own deaths, or that of our planet, sometimes our sense of immortality is shattered and the awareness of death comes through. Cronk engages with themes of ecological disaster throughout the poem both implicitly and explicitly. One stanza is peculiarly haunting:

are stepping on a million glass roaches.
The lady is busy all the time with
her brain tests.[40]

The glass roaches call to mind two ideas related to finitude: that cockroaches are reputed to be able to withstand a nuclear apocalypse, and that glass is formed over thousands of years from sand (i.e., obsidian). The conjunction of these two points in the image of the glass roaches reminds the reader of their relationship to death and dying. On one hand are creatures so hardy and tenacious that they can withstand almost any horror. On the other hand, they are being "stepp[ed] on" and are made from a substance that is fragile and easy to shatter. This leads us to the question of annihilation: If the planet were to die in an ecological disaster, what of the cockroach? The hardy, tenacious creatures that can withstand anything may not be able to withstand every version of planet death. This asks us to reconsider the nature of planet death. Perhaps our understanding of it only goes as far as our understanding of its impact on us. Some ecocritics believe that we should not consider planet death only in terms of its impact on human life, and posit that planet death is merely planet transmutation. Our inevitable deaths in such a situation could be seen as part of a bigger cycle.[41]

The second part of the stanza could be considered a gloss on the first. "The lady is busy all the time with / her brain tests" introduces a character type: the scientist. She is concerned with empirical data and is "busy," perhaps not engaging with the bigger issues. She projects her human desire to control what is essentially unknowable, wild, and free. This line is followed by "[w]e die and rush into the planet." The clear link between human death and the parasitical usage that the planet makes of

---

40 Ibid.

41 Voluntary Human Extinction Movement, http://vhemt.org/. The Voluntary Human Extinction Movement believe that human beings should stop reproducing in order to protect the planetary ecosystems that have been ravaged by human interventions. The members of the group have pledged not to reproduce themselves and they advocate that others do the same.

corpses as biological resources again recalls a redemptive version of necrophilia, a desire for the dead that is instinctual and deep.

The last few lines of the poem are eschatological and scatological. The entire poem reads like it takes place at the endtimes, but these last few lines especially echo the Book of Revelation with mentions of beasts, lizards, orgies, crowns, and shit:

> Lizard orgy.
> Seep. Seep.
> Crowns.
> mold spots &
> beasts taken &
>
> I've got all night for this shit.[42]

Cronk repurposes the apocalypse, as predicted in the Book of Revelation, for abject ends. By reducing the overarching narrative themes of Revelation to a handful of loaded and overdetermined words such as *beasts, lizard, crowns,* and *shit,* she reproduces the essence of the apocalypse and takes away any comfort of narrative, structure, or parable. Instead, she brings the reader horribly close to the Real: the lizard face beneath the niceties of story and structure.

Compare the "lizard orgy" from Cronk's poem with the dragon in Revelation 12: "And the earth helped the woman, and the earth opened her mouth, and swallowed up the flood which the dragon cast out of his mouth."[43] This exchange of bodily fluids between the dragon and the woman is a sexualized, hyperabject moment: a flood that can be both a marker of global warming and a release of sexual fluids emanates from the dragon. *Skin Horse* reads similarly to Revelation as an apocalyptic text and a revelation of the future — a future fueled by disgust, desire, and human destruction. The word beasts strongly connects *Skin*

---

42 Cronk, *Skin Horse.*
43 Revelation 12:16.

Horse to Revelation, which contains fifty-nine uses of the word. One of the most striking uses is in chapter 13: "Here is wisdom. Let him that hath understanding count the number of the beast: for it is the number of a man; and his number is Six hundred threescore and six."[44] This passage introduces the number of the beast as the infamous 666, a number that has passed into usage in schlocky horror stories and is used as simplistic shorthand for Satanic worship. Cronk's poem doesn't give context to the "beasts" she describes, but her use of the term in conjunction with references to lizards, orgies, crowns, and shit shows the text's overt play with the scatological and the eschatological, both of which are bound in the hyperabject. The indelible mark of the beast, the sign that horror is present, can be read with luminol theory to reveal crime scene and perpetrator through a series of indelible marks.

---

44 Revelation 13:18.

3. Christmas in Colorado

For everyone who's died in Colorado.
(It's never too late to write teen poetry.)
— Michael Du Plessis, *The Memoirs of*
JonBenét Ramsey by Kathy Acker

Christmas in Colorado is murder.

JonBenét died on Christmas Day, 1996, and never grew up to be a teenager. However, as if by magic, in Michael Du Plessis's *Memoirs,* JonBenét is gifted a new body, that of Tiffany. Yet like JonBenét, Tiffany dies in suspicious circumstances, while dressed in pink and tinsel and glitter and makeup, on a holiday, an occasion.

Tiffany is an important name in the recent history of Colorado. Matthew Murray murdered a young woman named Tiffany in 1997 in Colorado.[45] This fictional Tiffany is an instantiation of JonBenét: both of whom stand in for the victims in a series of atrocities against women in Colorado and beyond. Yet Tiffany dies not because she is murdered, but because she is ignorant. She dies a senseless, wasteful teenage death from a drug overdose in her absent parents' house. The chapter title "Tiffany Drowning in Ecstasy" has a double sense: that of her death from the combination of an ecstasy overdose and water toxicity, and an implicitly pornographic current that is culturally derived from her status as a pretty sixteen-year-old girl ripe for objectification. This chapter invokes the erotic dimension of the novella and offers Tiffany a redemptive release through death. By allowing her access to a blissed-out, inorganic state as an extension of her ecstasy-induced euphoria, Tiffany passes from childhood straight to death. She does not have to engage in the sexual, economic, marital, or social work expected of an adult woman. For Tiffany, all work, including the work of the body, has ceased.

---

45 As discussed in the preface, Tiffany Johnson was a young woman murdered by Matthew Murray at a mass shooting in Arvada, Colorado, in 2007.

Tiffany is presented as always-child and, more specifically, always-girl. She is dressed in pink glitter, with a tiara, sparkly nail polish, plastic high heels, and all the trashy pageantry of a sweet sixteen. Alongside birthday cupcakes and candy, Tiffany ingests six heart-shaped ecstasy pills. Her ignorance of the drug leads her to drink a massive quantity of water and die, a death that is imagined as drowning. In the act of dying, Tiffany becomes aligned with both the natural and artificial landscapes of Boulder:

> She's drowning, right here, on the carpet of her parents' living room in Boulder, Colorado, while the Boulder Creek rushes past outside. […] When you drown in Ecstasy, the last thought you have is, this is not so bad. Or rather, when you drown in a suburban living room in Boulder, Colorado, from the water you drank because you thought you should drink a lot of water with Ecstasy.[46]

This suspicious, unnecessary death of a young girl whose parents are irresponsibly absent reimagines and excavates the death of JonBenét. Tiffany relates the experience in second person: "You are presently drowning in your parents' living room, next to the sturdy Southwestern-style oak dinner table, glimpsing your reflection in the TV screen, black as a witch's mirror" and "on the beige wall-to-wall carpet, on your sixteenth birthday with your friends going "GET UP TIFFANY YOU'RE SCARING US WHAT'S WRONG? GET UP!"[47] At this stage of the narration, another kind of contraction is taking place, that of the bodily and the architectural. Buildings and characters meld. Tiffany is "drowning" in her parents' living room; she is becoming fused to the furniture, disappearing into the carpet as the "witch's mirror" of the television screen casts its otherworldly luminol glow on the scene.

For JonBenét, the life she reclaims, the teen years that Du Plessis magically bestows upon her, are banal and worthless.

---

46 Du Plessis, *Memoirs,* 81.
47 Ibid., 82.

In all of her guises in *Memoirs,* the character of JonBenét has a
sinister and inappropriate presence; she is a troubled teen who
dies repeatedly, inhabiting various bodies. The novella's epigraph, "For everyone who's died in Colorado. (It's never too late
to write teen poetry.)," sets its drily ironic tone, suggesting that
there is titillation to be found in the death of a young, beautiful
virgin, and that teen angst is not always worth the price. The
epigraph also signals playfully that the whole book is a kind of
previously unrealized sublimation of teen angst whose origins
lie in the nostalgic Boulder of DuPlessis's youth. This kind of
teen-fantasy death drive hinges on the cheapness and squalor of
life and the transcendent narcissism of the potential suicide. The
fictional JonBenét describes the claustrophobia of teenhood:

> Nothing happens under the thick plexiglass Colorado sky
> that domes this snowglobe in which I've become JonBenét.
> It's midday, and it's very warm, and I'm in a Boulder bath-
> room, with dingy floral linoleum and no windows. Bath-
> rooms never have windows in Boulder. But they do have
> mirrors, solid as the ones in mental hospitals, except that this
> mirror doesn't show anything of my perfect face.[48]

"Dingy floral linoleum" is used to invoke the abject parlor, the
idea of home as a place of death and horror. Though she employs
a very different tone, Kristeva likewise illustrates the horrors of
Auschwitz through the image of children's shoes and dolls under a Christmas tree. This contrast of innocence and violence
recalls the horror of child murder:

> In the dark halls of the museum that is now what remains
> of Auschwitz, I see a heap of children's shoes, or something
> like that, something I have already seen elsewhere, under a
> Christmas tree, dolls I believe. The abjection of Nazi crimes
> reaches its apex when death, which in any case, kills me, in-

---

48 Ibid., 4.

terferes with what, in my living universe, is supposed to save me from death: childhood, science among other things.[49]

Kristeva's abject response to the Nazi crimes recalled by the dolls under the Christmas tree is invoked through the Christmas snow globe in which JonBenét finds herself trapped. The ritual magic of childhood Christmases are compromised, sullied, and made sickening by the reminder of the annihilation of so many children at Auschwitz. This use of the camp to highlight the obscene is a tactic that Du Plessis uses over and over again in his conflation of the dead girl, the doll, and the snow globe, a tactic that falls into Kristeva's category of the abject.

The character of JonBenét tells us on the final page of *Memoirs*: "I see their little Christmas lights glowing and Boulder has never looked so much like toy town before. Snow Village. More landfill Americana for the twenty-first century. And they were hoping to keep me confined to the twentieth."[50] This inability to contain the murder of JonBenét in the twentieth century, this disastrous spillage of her presence into the twenty-first century, is the "true theatre" that Kristeva speaks about in her reading of the abject:

No, as in true theatre, without makeup or masks, refuse and corpses show me what I permanently thrust aside in order to live. These body fluids, this defilement, this shit, are what life withstands, hardly and with difficulty, on the part of death. There I am on the border of my condition as a living being.[51]

Alive, JonBenét was always presented theatrically. Almost no pictures of her exist without her platinum-blond dye job, her monstrous make-up, and her hoop-skirted polyester prom dresses. Yet the death of JonBenét as presented in the detailed, widely disseminated police reports on her mutilated body bring

49 Kristeva, *Powers of Horror*, 4.
50 Du Plessis, *Memoirs*, 98.
51 Kristeva, *Powers of Horror*, 3.

her into the realm of "refuse and corpses," the true theater that Kristeva speaks of. This uneasy ambivalence between purity and death makes JonBenét the perfect dead girl.

Among other things, *Memoirs* is an attempt to ameliorate the real death of a child by taking her beyond the pleasure principle. The real JonBenét Ramsey was not safe in the real Boulder, but the fictional JonBenét *is* safe in Du Plessis's fictional Boulder; she is already dead and cannot be hurt. Lisa Downing reminds us that in Freud's famous essay, "he postulates that the wish to return to an earlier, inorganic state is the primary and most pervasive drive of the human psyche."[52] JonBenét in her form as a plastic doll in *Memoirs* is a necro-fantasy. She is inorganic; she is passive; yet she is not dead; she has a voice. Du Plessis uses the trope of the dead girl to radically reimagine the clichéd perception of JonBenét as a doll-like sexual fantasy, a cipher for uncomfortable adult desires. He allows the dead JonBenét to ask questions that are stark and distressing: "Why am I dead?" and "Who killed me?"[53] Because these questions are addressed directly to us, the readers, we are implicated in her murder. According to Downing's psychoanalytic model of sexual maturation, we use necrophilia as a means by which to recognize our own deaths. Her model posits that the immature death drive of the pre-Oedipal child is displaced during unconscious formation and returns as necrophilia, which is used as a way to recognize one's own death through the death of the other.[54] We are acutely aware that in Du Plessis's novella JonBenét is attempting this recognition through confrontation with her own death. In this way, interacting with the character of JonBenét allows the reader to practice a form of redemptive necrophilia.

The fictional Colorado in *Memoirs* functions as a crime scene or a permanent shrine to the dead. Communion with the dead JonBenét, among others, is represented as a positive healing act. Du Plessis presents love as a queer strategy; in fact, the whole

---

52 Downing, *Desiring the Dead,* 47.

53 Du Plessis, *Memoirs,* 92.

54 Downing, *Desiring the Dead,* 47.

novella is a love letter to a dead girl who stands in for the male partner Du Plessis lost during his time in Colorado.[55] This is an example of redemptive necrophilia for both a dead girl and a queer relationship. Du Plessis wrote this book fifteen years after the 1996 death of JonBenét, in 2011. One of the characters in *Memoirs,* the Blue Fairy, explains that it is an "overblown break-up novel about Boulder that uses [JonBenét] as a metaphor."[56] This congruence of love story and murder story has a sticky logic that recreates the crime scene, Boulder, as the site of a teen love story and break-up. The insistence on using JonBenét as a metaphor is somewhat disingenuous as she is given autonomy and a strong voice — plural voices, in fact. She is no vacant cipher. The novella mirrors the ellipses and elisions in the real story of JonBenét, whose murder has never been solved. Another way in which Du Plessis positions JonBenét as a "body that matters" is by eschewing medical reports, morgue recordings, and other pitiless bodily markers in favor of reconnecting with and reclaiming the lost voice of the human child. Once a crime has been committed against a body, it is often the case that the medico-legal system will reproduce the crime through violent incursions into the privacy and integrity of the body and the person. Du Plessis refuses this hegemonic practice and allows JonBenét personhood and autonomy.

Another of JonBenét's bodies in the novel is that of the dead writer Kathy Acker. Du Plessis represents the fictional Acker as a doll that is "exactly twelve inches tall" and has "the string of a voice box hang[ing] down the back of her neck." The speeches the doll makes, however, are alien in the context of children's toys, which are not usually a site for radical political and sexual expression. [57] Du Plessis's decision to depict Acker as a talking

---

55 Janice Lee "An Interview with Michael Du Plessis," *Entropy,* March 24, 2014, https://www.entropymag.org/an-interview-with-michael-du-plessis.

56 Du Plessis, *Memoirs,* 93.

57 One interesting instance of a talking doll being used to advance progressive, feminist values was in the episode of *The Simpsons* titled "Lisa vs. Malibu Stacy" where Lisa Simpson helps to develop a talking doll which comes pre-loaded with phrases such as (15:22) "When I get married, I'm keeping my

doll[58] is an explicit reference to a short story Acker published
in 1990, "Dead Doll Humility," which is in turn a response to
Harold Robbins's attack on her for appropriating and repurpos-
ing a story of his in order to interrogate his racial and sexual
politics.[59] Acker's protagonist in "Dead Doll Humility," Capitol,
makes a doll that looks "exactly like herself" and functions as a
parodic version of the feminine ideal: "If you pressed a button
on one of the doll's cunt lips the doll said 'I am a good girl and
do exactly as I am told to do.'"[60] It is interesting that in Acker's
story the necessity to create such a doll comes when Capitol is
told by "prominent Black Mountains poets, mainly male" that
"a writer becomes a writer when and only when he finds his
own voice."[61] Acker makes a travesty of this by producing a doll
that represents Capitol's voice, and then having that voice con-
strained by the limitations of regulated femininity. Acker mentions that Capitol "didn't make any avant-garde poet dolls." Du
Plessis reverses this omission by returning Acker to life as just
that in his novella.

The overarching metaphor of the snow dome that houses
Boulder is a camp intervention that symbolizes the delicate
freezing of a perfect Christmas moment as much as it represents
claustrophobia and sterility. This fictionalized version of Boul-

own name" and (15:58) "Trust in yourself and you can achieve anything."
The Simpsons, "Lisa vs. Malibu Stacey." Episode 95. Directed by Jeff Lynch.
Written by Bill Oakley and Josh Weinstein. Fox, February 17, 1994.

58 Du Plessis, *Memoirs*, 71.

59 Kathy Acker, "Dead Doll Humility," *Postmodern Culture* 1, no. 1 (1990),
http://pmc.iath.virginia.edu/text-only/issue.990/acker.990. Paige Sweet explains that Acker wrote "Dead Doll Humility" "in response to the demand
made by Harold Robbins that she publically apologize for plagiarizing his
work. [...] By extracting Robbins's language and isolating specific linguistic
cells Acker reveals the delivery system responsible for transmitting sexual
and racial codes into narrative form: language." Paige Sweet, "Where's the
Booty? The Stakes of Textual and Economic Piracy as Seen through the
Work of Kathy Acker," *darkmatter* 5 (2009), http://www.darkmatter101.org/
site/2009/12/20/where%E2%80%99s-the-booty-the-stakes-of-textual-and-
economic-piracy-as-seen-through-the-work-of-kathy-acker/.

60 Acker, "Dead Doll Humility."

61 Ibid.

der is a permanent crime scene, a dead zone haunted equally by ghosts and by the ambivalence of the living. With no perpetrator found in the JonBenét case, guilt and suspicion attaches to everyone, to an entire community. The spatiality of this fictionalized Boulder, trapped under the plastic dome, enacts a punishment for the murder of JonBenét.

When luminol theory shines its light on the abject parlor, it reveals, it is magical, it is prescient, and it has a nasty allure.

Figure 4. Deadly Landscapes. Still from *The Luminol Reels*.

Deadly Landscapes
The *Locus Terribilis,* Colorado Gothic, *The Shining*

I believe that it is possible to claim the existence of a structure
of philosophy, *but unlike social structure, the structure of myth
or kinship structures, this structure does not relate to an original
or nuclear formal element, to any kind of basic cell that contains
the semantic and morphological data of the system. Instead, the
structure of "structural plastic analysis" should be understood
as a* result, *an a posteriori structure, a* residue of history.
— Catherine Malabou, *Plasticity at the Dusk of Writing:
Dialectic, Destruction, Deconstruction*

1. *The* Locus Terribilis

> *Chechnya: certainly that's a pastoral. Those*
> *people just have nothing but suicide.*
> —Joyelle McSweeney, *The Necropastoral*

Fictional Colorado under the plastic dome in Michael DuPlessis's *Memoirs* is a crystallised idyll, hermetically sealed, where violence has no release, and remains trapped. This pairing of idyllic natural beauty with violence, particularly sexual violence, can be traced back to Ovid, whose *Metamorphoses* contains meadows, grottos, and forests that form the backdrop to extreme sexual violence, traps where the dead must linger on, even after they have been the victims of trauma, abuse, and rape.

The trope of the *locus terribilis* or *locus inamoenus,* the "terrible or unpleasant place," arose from its opposite, the *locus amoenus,* or "pleasant place."[1] The ancient trope of the *locus amoenus* was prevalent in classical poetry, where it is strongly linked to the pastoral as it appears in the work of Horace, Virgil, and Seneca. The *locus amoenus* is a sylvan idyll that traditionally contains grass, trees, and water. Ovid later inverted this trope to create the *locus terribilis,* a place of natural beauty that hosts violence, rape, and murder. Daniel Garrison coined the term *locus inamoenus* in his article on Augustan literature, "The 'Locus Inamoenus': Another Part of the Forest."[2] Garrison traces this inversion to a specific historical incident: the battle between the Romans and the Eburones in 54 BCE. In this Northern European battle, the Romans suffered a great defeat that was partly attributed to the landscape. The thickets and bogs created the perfect conditions for a surprise attack against Caesar's troops.

By Augustan times, the period in which Ovid was writing, the *locus terribilis* was a "well-established topos, and one

---

1   I will use *locus terribilis* throughout as it carries a stronger sense of active horror than the negation in *locus inamoenus.* Lacan, "The Mirror-Phase as Formative of the Function of the I," 71–77.

2   Daniel Garrison, "The 'Locus Inamoenus': Another Part of the Forest," *Arion* 2, no. 1 (1992): 98–114.

that Seneca also used for his tragedy *Thyestes*."[3] Though Ovid didn't invent the motif, he certainly put it to the most inventive and sustained usage. Garrison illustrates this inventiveness by way of *Thyestes*. Seneca writes: "Throughout the forest a flame is wont to flicker, and high tree-trunks burn without fire. (673–75)"[4] Garrison contends, "These fireless flames may be literary exhalations of natural phenomena more common in the damp forests of northern Europe where decaying wood emits the eerie phosphorescent glow of foxfire, and decomposing organic matter gives off methane that burns with a bluish-yellow flame."[5] What Ovid does is to combine these two ideas to create a new "special effect," as Garrison describes it. Ovid does not pair frightening events with sinister locations, nor does he retreat into the sentimentality of Hellenic literature. Instead, his *Metamorphoses* contains several descriptions of sexual violence, torture, brutality, and murder that take place in beautiful, idyllic settings. These horrors are all the "more striking," according to Garrison, because they occur "in a pretty place that we lull ourselves into thinking is also a safe one."[6] Ovid often introduces a sacred grotto, a lush spring, a secret grove, or a dark and impenetrable forest to set a scene. Within these sublime, numinous spaces, he contaminates the landscape with violence and degradation. The spaces continue to be haunted by the violence committed there as the victims of the crimes do not disappear, but rather metamorphose into elements of the scene itself — from Myrrha's agonizing pregnancy while trapped in the form of a tree, to the terrified Callisto, who was transformed into a bear only to be hunted by her son.

The classical *locus amoenus* contains trees, water, and grass. In Ovid, there are several instances of this particular combina-

---

3   Ibid., 100. Ovid, writing in the first century CE, 2,000 years ago, was exiled for "carmen et error," or a poem and an error. He created decadent, brutal art that confronted the conservative regime of Emperor Augustus, and he and his material were excised from Rome.

4   Garrison, "The 'Locus Inamoenus,'" 101.

5   Ibid., 101.

6   Ibid., 100.

tion that signal danger and (often sexual) violence. An example of this can be seen in the episode of Salmacis and Hermaphrodite.[7] In this story Salmacis, a nymph who has broken away from the virgin-hunter Diana in order to live a life of sybaritic excess, rapes Hermaphrodite, son of Hermes and Aphrodite — the only example of rape by a nymph in classical mythology. The setting is a typical *locus amoenus* with grass, trees, and especially water functioning not only as setting but also as plot. According to Ovid, Hermaphrodite undresses and enters Salmacis's pool in order to bathe. Salmacis watches him from behind a tree and is overcome with lust for him. She enters the pool and forces herself upon him physically, calling out to the gods to join their flesh eternally. The gods honor this extremely sexually violent act, and the two are joined together in one body.[8]

Ovid's use of setting to signal danger is of peculiar relevance to luminol theory. The natural setting is a crime scene, a scene

---

7   The *Metamorphoses,* from which the story of Salmacis and Hermaphrodite is taken, was not the first of Ovid's works to introduce the trope of the *locus terribilis.* In fact, Ovid was working against an established pastoral tradition. In the earlier works of Latin poets Virgil and Horace the pastoral is closely related to sentimentality and nostalgia. Ovid's response to this tradition was to use landscapes to subvert their meanings for political effect. An earlier example of the *locus terribilis* in Ovid is present in his work the *Ars Amatoria.* In this book he explores the topography of Augustan Rome only to recall the violent history of the rape of the Sabines. He chose to avoid propaganda and sentimentality, though he still loved Rome dearly and was inconsolable with grief to be exiled by Augustus at the end of his life.

8   This is the origin of the word *hermaphrodite,* used frequently to describe people who identify as intersex. In her essay "Reading Ovid's Rapes," Amy Richlin asks, "How are we to read texts, like those of Ovid, that take pleasure in violence — a question that challenges not only the canon of Western literature but all representations. If the pornographic is that which converts living bodies into objects, such texts are certainly pornographic." Richlin goes on to describe in detail some of the *Metamorphoses'* "fifty tales of rape in its fifteen books," including those of women who were "transformed as a *punishment* for their rape and mutilation" — punished, that is, by the gods. Myrrha, Io, Callisto, and Medusa belong to this category, and Leucothoe and Perimele are murdered by their fathers (by proxy to the gods). Amy Richlin, "Reading Ovid's Rapes," in *Pornography and Representation in Greece and Rome,* ed. Amy Richlin (New York: Oxford University Press, 1992), 158–65.

of unimaginable terror for Hermaphrodite. Ovid describes the pool as hypernatural, a simulacrum of nature:

> No barren sedge grew there, no spiky rush;
> The water crystal clear, its margin ringed
> With living turf and verdure always green. (4.303ff.)[9]

This setting is at once fertile and sterile. The water is a symbol of generation but simultaneously does not sustain life of any kind. The surroundings that have been constructed are unnaturally perfect and anodyne; however, the fusty colour of the turf reveals excess, decay, and overstimulation. Charles Segal speaks about the Ovidian landscape as a place where "innocence is never preservable [...] where even the place of refuge and peace is invaded; there is no safety, no escape from arbitrary force."[10] The rape that occurs is *facilitated* by the beautiful location. The trees hide Salmacis from Hermaphrodite, allowing her ambush, and the water inflames her lust by revealing Hermaphrodite's naked body. It is the grass, however, that bears the most symbolic weight, its spookily beautiful "verdure" the unsettling clue that there is something wrong with the scene. While luminol testing is anachronistic, luminol theory can still be applied here. Ovid reports that the fountain is eternally cursed, that the bodily fluids that entered the water upon Hermaphrodite's rape cannot be removed. He tells us that there is a trace of the original crime in the water forever and that anyone who drinks the water will be affected:

> [...] "Dear father and mother, I pray you,
> grant this boon to the son who bears the names of you both:
> whoever enters this pool as a man, let him weaken as soon

---

9   Ovid, *Metamorphoses,* trans. A.D. Melville (Oxford: Oxford Paperbacks, 1998), 14.

10 Charles Segal, *Landscape in Ovid's Metamorphoses: A Study in the Transformations of a Literary Symbol* (Wiesbaden: F. Steiner Verlag, 1969).

as he touches the water and always emerge with his manhood
diminished!"
Venus and Mercury both were moved and fulfilled the prayer
of their androgyne son by infecting the pool with a neutering
tincture. (4.382–385)[11]

The scene retains a material trace of the original narrative that
cannot be removed, and that, further, is reactivated by an encounter with biological material. The *locus amoenus* becomes
the *locus terribilis,* a place of exquisite beauty that is both the
setting and the explicit facilitator of violence. Luminol theory
illuminates the flashes of horror that remain deep in the cursed
water, which is at once inviting and terrifying, hostile, hospitable, and haunted.

This blurring of the hostile and the hospitable, and the crime
scene and not-crime scene, that luminol theory illuminates is
exemplified in Jacques Derrida's portmanteau concept of *hostipitality,* which is used to demonstrate the collapsing of binaries
between etymologically related words.[12] Hosting, according to
Derrida, is etymologically associated with a range of contradic-
tory terms: *hostile, hospitality, ghost, hotel,* and *hostelry.* Derrida's essay can be considered a guide to viewing hostility and
hospitality as nonbinary, ambiguous concepts and to consider
what happens when natural locations become crime scenes.
These deeply uncanny, haunted landscapes pervert the classical notion of *xenia,* or hospitality. *Xenia* is a central concept in
ancient thinking and was considered a sacred principle whose
betrayal risked grave consequences from the gods. It is a mu-
tual bond: the guest who refuses *xenia* — or worse yet, betrays
it — in some way offends the gods as much as those who do not
offer proper *xenia.* The most obvious literary example of this

11 Ovid, *Metamorphoses: A New Verse Translation,* trans. David Raeburn
(London: Penguin Classics, 2004), 150.
12 Jacques Derrida, "Hostipitality," trans. Barry Stocker with Forbes Morlock,
Angelaki 5, no. 3 (2000): 3–18. Derrida wrote this article toward the end of
his life, and it exemplifies his method of excavating etymologies in order to
produce startling new meanings.

is the murder of Agamemnon by his wife Klytemnestra in his homecoming bath, an act that results in generations of *miasma,* or vengeance. The damaged spirits who throng Ovid's scenes are not afforded proper *xenia*; they are guests who have been mistreated and cannot leave.

One way to read the *locus terribilis* and use it to apply critical theory to contemporary literary works is to take *hostipitality* as a framework. Derrida discovers "troubling" meanings lurking inside: "*Hospitalität,* a word of Latin origin, of a troubled and troubling origin, a word which carries its own contradiction incorporated into it, a Latin word which allows itself to be parasitized by its opposite, 'hostility,' the undesirable guest [*hôte*] which it harbors as the self-contradiction in its own body."[13] *Guest, host, hostile,* and *ghost* are all enmeshed within this word. In the literary example of Klytemnestra, it is possible to see how she embodies this troubling range of meaning. On the surface, Klytemnestra offers *xenia* to Agamemnon by pouring him a bath, behaving as a host would. Yet soon after, she becomes hostile to him and he becomes her undesirable guest. When she murders him, he becomes a ghost, haunting generations of his family with miasma. In the same way, when Ovid presents idyllic settings as places that are at once desirable and deadly, their lushness is undercut by impending danger. He plays with the concept of the *locus terribilis* as a place of hosting and hostility, changing it to a place of enmity, violence, and horror. When Derrida argues that "hospitality is a self-contradictory concept and experience which can only self-destruct," he could be talking about Ovid's landscapes, which "self-destruct" in precisely this way.[14] It is the ambiguity between hospitality and hostility that creates the Ovidian thrill and which turns the *locus terribilis* into a crime scene. *Hostipitality* can also be understood as a way of thinking through luminol. Luminol excavates and, more specifically, illuminates the horror beneath even the most beautiful surface. In the same way, *hostipitality* always reminds us of

---

13 Ibid., 3.
14 Ibid., 5.

the hostility at the heart of the guest-host exchange and of the ghostly luminol trace that remains.

Hostipitality can also account for the uneasy and contaminatory relationship between host and parasite. The crime scene is riddled with bacteria, fungus, and spores bursting from decomposing bodies. Contamination at the crime scene is inevitable. Pandemics such as the great plague of Athens in 430 BCE, the devastating influenza outbreak of 1918, and the Ebola crisis of 2014 turn whole nations, and indeed international zones, into scenes full of dead and dying people who are partially or wholly buried and transmitting horror and disease. Forensic anthropologists are able to discover information as to the kinds of violence that have taken place by analyzing human remains and other artifacts at mass graves, often revealing cultic or ritual material.

In Lucretius's account of the formation of the earth, he describes the land itself roiling with "a great abundance of heat and moisture" and how "wombs would grow, holding to the earth by roots." This disgusting image is compounded by a Kristevan image of how "nature would direct thither pores of the earth and make it discharge from these open veins a liquid like to milk."[15] The earth in Lucretius's formation is both generative and obscene. There is no "border between inside and outside," and the earth itself is a "supersaturated, leaking membrane."[16] Later passages of Lucretius describe in great, loving detail the symptoms of plague and disease using terms such as "clogged," "oozed with blood," "burning," "thirsting," and "trembling."[17] The earth itself is responsible for the transmission of disease, with every creature affected. The countryside is equally dangerous, with no

---

15 Lucretius, *On the Nature of Things,* trans. W.H.D. Rouse, rev. Martin F. Smith (1924; Cambridge: Harvard University Press, 1975), 443.

16 Kristeva, *Powers of Horror,* 53; Joyelle McSweeney, "Can the Necropastoral Be Political?," *Montevidayo*, January 31, 2011, http://www.montevidayo.com/can-the-necropastoral-be-political.

17 Lucretius, *On the Nature of Things,* 579–83.

chance of a "permanent, separated rural peace."[18] This poetics of annihilation imagines the entire earth scattered with corpses:

> Many in public places and roads you might see all about, bodies half-dead with fainting limbs caked with squalor and covered in rags, perishing in filth of body […] all the temples of the celestials everywhere remained burdened with corpses, all which places the sacristans had crowded with guests […] they would lay their own kindred amidst loud lamentation upon piles of wood not their own, and would set light to the fire, often brawling with much shedding of blood rather than abandon the bodies.[19]

These are the very final words of Lucretius's poem, cut off suddenly and without warning, serving to heighten their effect. Here he describes how hard people fought in times of utter extremity to provide proper burial to their kin, or as proper a burial as they could manage under the circumstances of universal plague and horror. Such was the importance of ritual burial that there was "much shedding of blood" to protect the right of families to bury their dead. In spite of fears of contamination and the very real threat of transmitting disease, still the ritual remained.

Whilst the plague was the disease that informed Ovid's writing, as the most terrifying example of a pandemic in ancient times, Colorado Gothic arises from another form of bacterial invasion, the so-called "white plague,"[20] that most Gothic of illnesses which briefly turned Colorado into "the world's sanatorium"[21] — tuberculosis.

---

18 McSweeney, "Can the Necropastoral Be Political?."

19 Lucretius, *On the Nature of Things,* 591.

20 Louie Croft Boyd, "The Tuberculosis Situation in Denver, Colorado," *American Journal of Nursing* 7, no. 4 (1907): 265–68, at 265.

21 Shanna Lewis, "How Tuberculosis Fueled Colorado's Growth," *Colorado Matters,* Colorado Public Radio Website, February 10, 2015, http://www.cpr.org/news/story/how-tuberculosis-fueled-colorados-growth

2. Colorado Gothic

> *The Church is laid out so that the parishioners are facing west. In the center of the pulpit is a twenty-foot wide, forty-foot high window that faces the Rocky Mountains. During services, the window is sometimes fully covered with a curtain, When the curtain is opened, congregants are exposed to an unobstructed view of the Rocky Mountains, in front of which is superimposed a simple outline of a cross.*
> — Robert W. Larkin, "Comprehending Columbine"

The state of Colorado is exquisitely beautiful: set in the Rocky Mountains, it is a popular holiday destination for wealthy skiers who are drawn to its clean air and fresh snow. Yet in this setting of such natural beauty, there have been an unusually high number of globally famous crimes. In the last twenty-five years there have been several major crimes in the state — most notoriously the Columbine massacre, the most widely discussed mass shooting of all time. Ted Bundy, one of the most prolific and culturally relevant serial killers on record, perpetrated several crimes in Colorado. Further back, the state was founded on the originary genocide of indigenous people in the Sand Creek massacre of 1864. The state's violent history has drawn many writers of fiction and nonfiction to base their violent crime stories in the state, including the most famous horror writer of all, Stephen King. The state itself, built on originary genocide, is a palimpsestic crime scene that, once illuminated, reveals occulted fictional and true crimes.

The overlaying of contemporary crimes onto national violence is the subject of much of American Gothic and, though there have been a huge amount of globally notorious crimes in many (perhaps all) states, Colorado has its own spooky imaginary and local peculiarities. It is this "Colorado Gothic" that marks out the state as distinct from, for example, "Texas Gothic," "Appalachian Gothic," or, perhaps most widely represented in literature, film and media, "California Gothic." It is the idyllic nature of Colorado that makes it the perfect example of the *locus terribilis,* the violent idyll.

Colorado is home to several "fervor churches" which origi-
nated in the 1990s. Dave Cullen in his book on the Columbine
massacre describes the statewide religious hysteria that char-
acterized Colorado: "Since pioneer days and the Second Great
Awakening, Colorado had been a hotbed on the itinerant min-
istry circuit"; "by the 1990s, Colorado Springs was christened
the Evangelical Vatican. The city of Denver seemed immune to
the fervor, but its western suburbs were roiling."[22] The epigraph
to this chapter describes the way in which the natural beauty of
Colorado is incorporated into the drama and ritual of evangelical church services, where "forty-foot high"[23] windows open out
on to the Rocky Mountains, as though they were designed as a
backdrop for services. This particularity suggests that the location for worship is carefully chosen by church architects in order
to suggest a causal link between God and nature, and between
the supernatural power of religion and the Colorado landscape.
In the Stanley Kubrick version of *The Shining,* discussed in more
detail below, when the Torrance family are headed towards the
Overlook Hotel, high in the Rocky Mountains, Wendy Torrance
asks her husband Jack "wasn't it around here that the Donner
Party got stranded?"[24] to which he replies that it was 'Farther
West, in the Sierras."[25] This is an important discussion as *The
Shining* is a story about a family who travel west for a better
life, only to end in horrific tragedy and as they travel they re-
member the Donner Party who embodied the "common mid-
nineteenth-century American dream — a better life to be found
by going west" a dream that ends in brutal hypothermia and
cannibalism. This dream, like any American Dream, is predicated on stolen land and the drive to colonise. *The Shining* as
imagined by Stanley Kubrick does not shy away from that aspect of American Gothic, but rather brings the audience into
close and uncomfortable proximity with the racist origins of

---

22 Dave Cullen, *Columbine* (London: Old Street Publishing, 2009), 103–4.

23 Ibid., 17–18.

24 Stanley Kubrick (dir.), *The Shining,* 1980.

25 Ibid.

the United States. By invoking the Donner Party in the early stages of the film, and by transplanting them from the Californian Gothic to the Colorado Gothic, Kubrick shows how even stories that do not rightly belong in the geographical bounds of the state leave their traces on the frozen imaginary of the Rockies. The horrific science of the Donner Party's deaths also has a grisly echo with Jack Torrance's eventual hypothermic fate as his wife and child escape with their lives. According to Donald K. Grayson in his anthropological study of the Donner Party deaths: "under cold stress, inactive males also suffer greater core temperature reduction than inactive females" and "adult women, and to some extent, subadult females should fare better under conditions marked by famine and/or extreme cold than their male counterparts."[26] This is certainly true for Wendy, who leaves Jack frozen and howling as she escapes with their toddler son, Danny. As she leaves Jack to the fate that befell so many of the Donner men, Kubrick brings the narrative full circle, by firmly planting that corrupt American Dream in the snows of Colorado.

Writing in 1907, the year that the Overlook was purported to be built, Louie Croft Boyd wrote of conditions in Colorado as it became home to a tubercular "vast army of sufferers which other sections of the country are pouring into Colorado" and which only intensified the "crowded conditions and unsanitary dwelling-places."[27] Though patients were "admitted to the County Hospital" they were "not desired" and, in fact, the "majority of the patients live in tents." In order to attempt to police and regulate the refugees who arrived in the state to take advantage of clean, fresh air, laws were passed stating that "expectoration in public places is prohibited by law."[28] This attempt to police bodies, to construct a cordon sanitaire between the diseased and the healthy also created a hierarchy between residents and refugees.

---

26 Donald K. Grayson, "Donner Party Deaths: A Demographic Assessment," *Journal of Anthropological Research* 46, no. 3 (1990): 223–42, at 233.

27 Louie Croft Boyd, "The Tuberculosis Situation in Denver, Colorado," 265.

28 Ibid., 266.

Colorado Gothic, then, occupies this uneasy space between purity and contamination, the clear, mountain atmosphere presenting a frozen stasis, whilst trapping and preserving the "roiling,"[29] bacterial chaos below. This this peculiar *locus terribilis* has been the setting for some of the most globally-notorious crimes of recent history.

Three years following the unsolved murder of JonBenét Ramsey, Colorado was in news headlines the world over for one of the most shocking mass murders and school shootings of all time: Columbine. In April 1999 Eric Harris and Dylan Klebold entered Columbine High School, where they were enrolled as students, shot and murdered twelve students and a teacher, and injured twenty-one others. After terrorizing staff and students for several hours, they committed suicide. In addition to the shootings, they planted almost one hundred homemade explosives throughout the school grounds. The massacre was the deadliest school shooting to date, and its consequences included major national and international debates about firearm control and teenage mental health. These debates had a lasting impact on the school system, policing, and gun control in the US. Klebold and Harris explicitly cited Timothy McVeigh, the 1995 Oklahoma City bomber, as an inspiration.[30] In turn, Columbine has been linked to over thirty subsequent mass murder cases.[31] Dave Cullen, a reporter who attended the scene at Columbine, writes in his account of the case:

---

29 Cullen, *Columbine*, 103–4.

30 The date of the Columbine shooting was April 20, 1999, one day after the April 19 anniversary of the Oklahoma City attack.

31 According to criminologist Ralph W. Larkin, of the twelve school shootings that took place in the US in the ten years after Columbine (1999–2009), eight of the murderers were explicitly inspired by Harris and Klebold: T.J. Solomon in Conyers, Georgia; Seth Trickley in Fort Gibson, Oklahoma; Charles Andrew Williams in Santee, California; John William Romano in East Greenbush, New York; Jon Wiese in Red Lake, Minnesota; James Newman in Reno, Nevada; Alvaro Castillo in Hillsborough, North Carolina; and Cho Seung-Hui in Blacksburg, Virginia. Ralph W. Larkin, "The Columbine Legacy: Rampage Shootings as Political Acts," *American Behavioral Scientist* 52, no. 9 (2009): 1309–26.

It's a safe bet that Eric and Dylan watched the carnage of Waco and Oklahoma City on television, with the rest of the country. Those atrocities were particularly prominent in this region. McVeigh was tried in federal court in downtown Denver and sentenced to death while the boys attended Columbine in the suburbs. The scenes of devastation were played over and over. In his journal, Eric would brag about topping McVeigh. Oklahoma City was a one-note performance: McVeigh set his timer and walked away; he didn't even see his spectacle unfold. Eric dreamed much bigger than that.[32]

Though this is a highly speculative account, it does illuminate two relevant points. First, Cullen, a native of Colorado, describes mass atrocities, even those perpetrated beyond the borders of the state, as "prominent in this region," an assertion supported by the fact that McVeigh, perpetrator of the largest act of domestic terrorism in US history, had his lengthy and painful trial in the state of Colorado. Second, Cullen notes the references in Harris's journal both to McVeigh and to Harris's desire to "top" him and watch the "spectacle unfold." Both of these points indicate that the context was relevant to the crime (the spectacle of the trial as it unfolded in Colorado) and also that the killers, or at least Harris, was interested in perpetrating the crime specifically within Colorado. He wanted to stay and watch (the visual image of the "spectacle") what their crime did to the people they murdered and injured as well as to the environment of Columbine and, by extension, Colorado. This incident reverberated through Colorado and through the world, where, after Columbine, mass murders are more prevalent than ever.

Mass killings are not the only major crimes of national and international interest that have occurred in the state. Bundy, one of the most notorious serial killers in the world, came to Colorado in January 1975. By April he had murdered three young women: Caryn Campbell, Julie Cunningham, and Denise Oliverson. Though he perpetrated his crimes throughout the US,

---

32 Cullen, *Columbine*, 10–11.

the crimes in Colorado have taken on a grimy valence — particularly the murder of Cunningham, in Vail, Colorado. She was brutally murdered by Bundy after, he testified, he tricked her into carrying his ski boots for him by feigning injury.[33] This particular ruse has been popularized in several cultural representations of Bundy and is part of serial-killer folklore.[34] In this case the Colorado landscape participated in the crime, with the snow-covered Vail Mountain offering an alibi both for the heavy ski boots and the injury. When excavated with luminol theory, the murder of Cunningham reveals the mythic narrative that haunts and occupies Bundy's other crimes. It shines through the snow scene to reveal not only the individual crimes of abduction, murder, rape, and necrophilia, but also the systemic patriarchal crimes perpetrated against women both in reality and in cultural representation.

By limning the crime scene of Colorado, luminol theory reveals histories occulted below the state's most famous crimes. The careful analyst can take the fragmented, seemingly inchoate crimes and illuminate them in order to curate the state of Colorado and reveal it as not only a crime scene but *the* crime scene, a microcosm of and genesis for other US crime scenes. Columbine is the ur-school shooting, JonBenét's killing the most famous US child murder of all time, and Bundy's crimes are amongst the most vividly resonant in the national true-crime imaginary. Yet these major crimes are only a part of the story to be limned.

Below the news headlines and saturated images are weirder, ghostly traces of the state of Colorado as a constellation point for horror of all kinds. The crimes I discuss here were influenced by, and have influenced, a whole range of mystic, religious, and otherworldly practices.

---

33 "Colorado Bureau of Investigation Cold Case File: Julie L. Cunningham" https://apps.colorado.gov/apps/coldcase/casedetail.html?id=2421.

34 Perhaps the most famous of these cultural representations is that of Buffalo Bill in Thomas Harris's 1988 novel and Jonathan Demme's 1991 film *The Silence of the Lambs*. *Forced Entry* (dir. Lizzy Borden, 2002), a Gonzo porn film based loosely on the serial killer Richard Ramirez, has a scene that features a ruse similar to the one used on Cunningham.

Robert Mighall reminds us that the genocidal origins of the United States are always "what lies beneath" the contemporary American horror story:

"Gloomy wrong," guilt and nemesis are the master-plots of American Gothic. It is a big paranoid country, guiltily aware that it has taken the land away from people, and taken other people away from their lands: hence the symbolic importance of land, and what lies beneath it, in fictions from [Nathaniel] Hawthorne to Stephen King. The Indian burial grounds that lie beneath the haunted edifices in *The Shining* (1980), and *The Amityville Horror* (1979) and *Poltergeist* (1982) entail indelible stains of guilty horror that erupt to damn the new masters of this nation.[35]

The twin specters of colonization and slavery are never far from the surface in the American narrative, and particularly in the American crime narrative. At Sand Creek, Colorado, Colonel John Chivington was successful in his genocidal attack at least in part because of his promise to the indigenous community that they would be safe under his protection:

Pre-dawn came with a fright on November 29, 1864, as mainly Colorado militia, seven-hundred soldiers in all, attacked an undefended Indian camp on Sand Creek. […] Those slaughtered were babies, old men, women, and children. The majority of the able-bodied men were on a hunting trip. Black Kettle and his people had been told they would be safe on this reservation.[36]

The massacre was murder on a massive scale and it was military in character, but it was also a personal betrayal characterised

---

35 Robert Mighall, "Gothic Cities," in *The Routledge Companion to Gothic*, eds. Catherine Spooner and Emma McEvoy, 54–72 (Abingdon: Routledge, 2007), 58.

36 Don and Kellie Rainwater, *The Dark Side of Colorado: Murder, Mayhem, and Massacre* (CreateSpace Independent Publishing Platform, 2008), 8.

by pathological annihilatory violence, based on Chivington's personal ignorance and fear of indigenous people. This disgust allowed Chivington to justify and perpetrate violence in the eugenic drive for purity. Yet this purity can only ever be illusory, predicated as it is on genocidal atrocities committed on marginalised bodies. In the Colorado Gothic ur-text, *The Shining*, Kubrick's radical reimagining of King's novel shifts it away from being a generic horror story, and into cold, banal, proximity with real historical violence, violence such as that perpetrated by Chivington.

3. The Shining

> *People are squeamish about art about violence and suffering*
> *that remains art-sy. Art about disasters should be transparent; to*
> *foreground the art, the pageantry is somehow offensive. You are*
> *accused of "aestheticizing" suffering, violence, torture etc. — as if*
> *that is an inherently negative thing, as if that makes it flippant,*
> *as if that is not pious enough. As if the art itself is a crime.*
> — Johannes Göransson, "'Why Is the Poem Such an
> Insult to This Evil Life?' On Sandy Hook, Blake
> Butler, Aase Berg, and Disaster Aesthetics"

Stephen King's *The Shining* and Stanley Kubrick's later film adaptation of the novel limn Colorado as a crime scene in a powerful and cohesive way. These texts, but most particularly Kubrick's film version, have excited a range of critical, theoretical, and audience responses that far exceed their statuses as works of fiction. *The Shining* evidently taps into deep cultural anxieties around the state of Colorado specifically and the territory of the United States generally. In turn, *The Shining* is an important intertext, or even ur-text, for Du Plessis's *Memoirs*. This particular palimpsest of Colorado fictions can be excavated with luminol theory, its glow illuminating the heads of the terrorized protagonists — children with luminous white hair.[37]

There are three versions of *The Shining*: Stephen King's 1977 novel,[38] Stanley Kubrick's 1980 film,[39] and Stephen King's 1997 miniseries,[40] created by him in an attempt to wrest back control over a project that had transcended its origins to become a phenomenal cult classic in the hands of Kubrick. This eventual reputation was slow in developing, and in the year that the film

---

37 Horror has several examples of the supernatural white-haired child. A famous example is John Wyndham, *The Midwich Cuckoos* (London: Penguin, 2008); its film adaptation *Village of the Damned* (dir. Wolf Rilla, 1960); and John Carpenter's eponymous 1995 remake of that adaptation.

38 Stephen King, *The Shining* (1977; London: Hodder Paperbacks, 2011).

39 Stanley Kubrick (dir.), *The Shining*, 1980.

40 Mick Garris (dir.), *The Shining*, 1997.

version was released, several serious film critics were scathing of the transformative work that Kubrick had performed, taking King's straightforwardly supernatural ghost story and turning it into a work of psychological terror that defied categorization. Stephen King "conducted a press campaign against Kubrick's adaptation. 'You know what?' King asked. 'I think he wants to hurt people with this movie. I think he really wants to make a movie that will hurt people.' In *Danse Macabre,* his 1981 critical reflections on horror, King called the film 'maddening, perverse, and disappointing.'"[41] Though the miniseries remains part of the palimpsestic text of *The Shining,* it is of less interest in this chapter, and I will primarily be referring to the novel and the film.

The Shining, in each instantiation, tells the story of Jack Torrance (played by Jack Nicholson in the film), a failed writer, failed teacher, and failed husband who recovers from his alcoholism and despair long enough to agree to a job caretaking the Overlook Hotel in the Rocky Mountains over a brutal winter season. Cabin fever gradually sets in and his mind disintegrates, he returns to drinking, and he decides to kill his wife, Wendy (Shelley Duvall), and Danny (Danny Lloyd), their toddler son. During the course of the winter both Jack and Danny see traces of previous horror in the abandoned hotel, with Danny's gift of "the shining" allowing him direct access to the Real. Blood and corpses surface in the empty rooms as Danny's ability to "shine" acts as a highly effective form of luminol.

However, as Mark Fisher notes in his article "You Have Always Been the Caretaker: The Spectral Spaces of the Overlook Hotel," the Overlook is a "leisure hive built on top of an Indian Burial Ground (this detail was added by Kubrick); a potent image of a culture founded upon (the repression of) the genocide of the native peoples."[42] Mark Fisher reads the two *Shining* texts (the film and the novel, but not the miniseries) as "one intercon-

---

41 Roger Luckhurst, *The Shining* (London: BFI Classics, 2013), 8.
42 Ibid.

nected textual labyrinth,"[43] yet he finds this distinction in Kubrick's version important enough to comment on, as it shows
"what haunts America" according to Roger Luckhurst, which "is
a violent history — the settlers who systematically murdered the
Native Americans, built wealth on the backs of African slaves,
and suffered the parricidal guilt of a rebellious colony that shook
off the colonial father to become an independent republic in the
War of Independence."[44] Even if we accept that Kubrick seeks to
bring *The Shining* into closer proximity with its genocidal histories, he still perpetuates the racist myth of the "magical negro" in
his direction of Scatman Crothers as Dick Halloran, the hotel's
chef. Hallorann, an African American character, exists merely
to save the white characters.[45]

On the day the family arrives at the Overlook, Hallorann is
about to leave for Florida for the winter months. He tells Danny,
"What you got, son, I call it shinin' on, the Bible calls it having
visions, and there's scientists that call it precognition. I've read
up on it, son. I've studied on it. They all mean seeing the future.
Do you understand that?"[46] Here he is also explaining the supernatural phenomenon to the reader. "Shining" refers to an ability
to pick up on atmospheres, moods, and the thoughts of the people around those who have the gift, as well as an ability to read
the future through visions or hallucinations. In the novel, the
gift is almost exclusively confined to revealing what is dangerous
and deadly: blood streaming from the elevators into the lobby,
twin girls chopped into gory pieces, the word REDRUM (murder)
scrawled on a mirror. The metaphor of shining as a means to excavate hidden crime narratives is a microcosmic example of the
function of luminol theory. Luminol theory allows the careful

---

43 Mark Fisher, "You Have Always Been the Caretaker: The Spectral Spaces
of the Overlook Hotel," *Perforations* 29 (2007), http://www.pd.org/Perfora-
tions/perf29/mfi.pdf.

44 Luckhurst, *The Shining*, 43.

45 For more on this trope, see Matthew W. Hughey, "Cinethetic Racism: White
Redemption and Black Stereotypes in 'Magical Negro' Films," *Social Problems* 56, no. 3 (2009): 543–77.

46 King, *The Shining*, 61.

reader to piece together multiple hidden narratives within *The Shining*. For example, to train Danny's "shine" on occulted crime narratives, the reader can trace luminol through the novel. Early in the story, while Danny is still residing in Boulder, he has a premonition of the final scenes at the Overlook, when his father attacks Danny and Wendy with an axe: "Now the snow was covering the shingles. It was covering everything. A green witchlight glowed into being on the front of the building, flickered, and became a giant, grinning skull over two crossed bones."[47] The green glow of the "witchlight" is overlaid upon the scene to warn Danny that he is in severe danger. The future and present collide, a palimpsest rendered legible through the application of a glow eerily reminiscent of luminol.

Before his departure, Hallorann shows the Torrances how to survive the winter in practical terms, by giving them a tour of the kitchen and showing them the provisions he has left for them, and metaphysically, by alerting Danny to a supernatural means of calling for Dick's help by "shining." This scene coalesces around the vast hotel kitchen. It is no accident that both practical and supernatural advice is dispensed as the group wanders around the pantry and the walk in-freezer,[48] and finally arrives at the gas burner: "'I love gas,' [Hallorann] said, and turned on

---

47 Ibid., 23.

48 Elissa Marder, a psychoanalytic scholar, writes about a case in which a mother was found to have hidden her dead babies in the family freezer. This action, Marder argues, was the mother's attempt to safeguard rather than destroy the children that she was psychologically unable to deal with. This case can be read against later scenes in *The Shining* where Jack Torrance freezes to death, kept safe from hurting himself or others. In psychoanalytic terms, "[a] freezer is, after all, itself a particular kind of a case — a technologically enhanced object designed for holding, containing, or preserving something (normally food) against the ravages of time. A freezer is designed to keep something safe, protected and near. In this sense it is the opposite of a disposal site; it retains, contains, and safeguards the objects that are confined in it. It is also the opposite of an oven. Following this association, dead babies in the freezer might be read as a reversal of the common image of the pregnant woman who has 'buns in the oven.'" Elissa Marder, *The Mother in the Age of Mechanical Reproduction: Psychoanalysis, Photography, Deconstruction* (New York: Fordham University Press, 2012), 25.

one of the burners. Blue flame popped into life and he adjusted it down to a faint glow with a delicate touch. 'I like to be able to see the flame you're cookin' with. You see where all the surface burner switches are?'"[49] In offering practical advice, Hallorann also uses a blue glow, in this case that of the gas burner, to invoke warmth, security, and comfort and to remind Danny of his own ongoing protective presence. Finally, toward the end of the novel, Danny is alerted to a glow in his father's eyes in an acute, desperate moment: "It was Jack and yet not Jack. His eyes were lit with a vacant, murderous glow; his familiar mouth now wore a quivering, joyless grin."[50] The green glow of the witchlight and the blue glow of the gas have become "vacant" and "murderous" in his father's eyes, alerting Danny to the fact that Jack is no longer there and that he must escape his murderous intent.

Fisher applies a hauntological reading to *The Shining*, uncovering archaeological meaning through the layers of repression built into the text. He specifically mentions spectrality and haunting, saying, "Haunting happens when a space is invaded or otherwise disrupted by a time that is out-of-joint, a dyschronia," and stating that *The Shining* is "fundamentally concerned with the question of repetition."[51] This repetition in a minor sense relates to the microcosmic murder of the family — first when Mr. Grady (Philip Stone), an erstwhile caretaker of the Overlook, kills his wife and daughters, and then Jack's attempt to recreate that murder. In a wider sense, the repetition relates to the violence and terror that recur at the site of the Overlook Hotel, including organized crime, murders, suicides, and even mass killings.

Perhaps the most interesting application of the hauntological is in Fisher's reading of Jack, who represents "an appalling structural fatality, a spectral determinism. To have 'always been the caretaker' is never to have been a subject in his own right. Jack has only ever stood in for the Symbolic and the homicidal

49 King, *The Shining*, 51.
50 Ibid., 301.
51 Ibid.

violence which is the Symbolic's obscene underside."[52] Jack has "always been the caretaker," and he has always lived in Colorado. He was involved in its genealogy of brutalities, from the Sand Creek massacre of 1864 to the murder of Grady's daughters. If he has always been the caretaker, the obscene father, the structural, patriarchal, colonial enforcer, then who has been his perennial victim? When we witness Danny, an innocent blond child, trapped in a family home, in the snow, with his potential murderer, perhaps there is more than a spectral foreshadowing of Christmas Day, 1996, but as well as the later attempted murders of his own family, we also see that the Overlook is peopled entirely by ghosts, ghosts who emerged around the turn of the century when the Overlook was built. When discussing the Ahwahnee Hotel, features of which were used by Kubrick in designing the Overlook, Roger Luckhurst says of the great hall:

> We are invited to read the cues of the room historically, and clearly in relation to the violent history of the American frontier and the destruction of the Native Americans. The Overlook was built between 1907 and 1909, Ullman explains in another tracking shot along the exterior of the hotel, "and I believe they actually had to repel a few Indian attacks as they were building it." (The Ahwahnee Hotel was built on the site of an indigenous Miwok village, rudely incorporating the designs of the culture it effaced.)[53]

This indexical connection between real violence perpetrated against the Miwok village, and the American Gothic trope of "gloomy wrong"[54] produced by proximity to colonial and genocidal histories are brought together in this room. There is a scene of unaccountable and sudden violence between Jack and Wendy in this room, a violence that foreshadows an escalation of horrors and that ends in near-annihilation for the hotel and

---

52 Ibid.

53 Luckhurst, *The Shining,* 43.

54 Mighall, "Gothic Cities," 58.

its inhabitants. It may be a stretch to suggest that Kubrick might have been "specifically aware of the growing Native American activism of the 1970s," but it feels valid to suggest that "If there is a deliberate semiotic echo of these events in *The Shining,* Kubrick does it obliquely, in the deep space of the design, rather than exploiting the melodrama of undead vengeance of Native spirits."[55] Jack's role as caretaker is nothing more than a pretext for oppression and rage; his chaotic and unpredictable rule a microcosm of colonial, patriarchal enforcement, the room a material reminder of genocide and imperialism.

Kubrick takes King's Gothic novel, and brings it into closer proximity with the true American Gothic, the story of indigenous genocide and stolen land. Du Plessis, in his later Colorado Gothic novel Memoirs, demonstrated that he was aware of Colorado histories, and of his intertexts, including Kathy Acker's "Dead Doll Humility," *The Shining,* and another King-authored novel set in Boulder, *The Stand,* in the writing of *Memoirs.* Du Plessis clearly takes serious issue with King's version of *The Shining,* as evidenced in the harangue delivered by Kathy Acker (discussed below). Though never directly referencing his preference for Kubrick's version, blond, magical Danny and the bloody-velvet-dress–wearing twins of the Overlook become reference points for the blond, magical, prettily dressed, and undead JonBenét. She haunts the novel, she haunts Boulder, and she haunts our imaginations. Perhaps we could consider Fisher's formulation of Jack as the caretaker who stands in for homicidal violence and cast JonBenét — real, mythical, and imagined — as someone who has always been the victim, the corollary to Colorado's "dark side." Yet in *Memoirs,* Du Plessis reclaims JonBenét from this role. Yes, she repeats, and yes, she is the token of the return of the repressed, but she is given autonomy, a voice, and a young adulthood, and she transcends her status as beautiful dead doll, as white, blond corpse.

In *Memoirs,* Du Plessis explicitly ties the two murder narratives together. An entire chapter consists of the character Kathy

---

55 Luckhurst, *The Shining,* 45–46.

Acker offering a disquisition on a writer named Stephen King, who, like her and the protagonist of *Memoirs,* JonBenét, is a fictional version of the real figure of the same name. There is an obvious link between Du Plessis's book, which is described as an "overblown break-up novel about Boulder that uses [JonBenét] as a metaphor"[56] and King's novel and Kubrick's film, which are really about Colorado. The two versions of *The Shining* are murder mysteries that focus on genocide, the Depression, and gendered violence through the psychological horror story of a single family. Danny, Wendy, and Jack are the metaphor; Colorado is the subject.

In the introduction to *Memoirs,* Peggy Kamuf focuses on chapter 9, "Why Stephen King Writes Such Bad Novels." In this chapter the character of Kathy Acker gives a lecture at "the university" and faces resistance from a group of Boulder locals who support King as an ex-resident. Kathy Acker inflames the crowd, saying, "Stephen King isn't just a bad novelist, crappy, derivative, moralistic, unimaginative, limited. He's a bad writer, an evil one,"[57] and, "Stephen King is evil like Boulder and Boulder is evil like Stephen King! Don't think I haven't seen through the little understanding the two of you have going on." Her speech builds hysterically, and her conspiracy theory about King becomes extreme. All other American authors are mere pseudonyms for King; Boulder is "nothing but a debased solar cult that uses King's works to transmute and transmit everything into Boulder,"[58] and finally, "All of Stephen King's works make up a secret psychogeography of Boulder."[59] This is an intentionally bizarre and over-the-top scene it is at the end of it that Acker's character is revealed to be a twelve-inch-tall doll"[60] and Du Plessis uses it to contextualize and to some extent parody the conspiracy theories, critical inquiries, and psychoanalytic

---

56 Du Plessis, *Memoirs,* 96.

57 Ibid., 69.

58 Ibid., 71.

59 Ibid.

60 Ibid., 75.

readings that proliferate around *The Shining*, both the novel and the Kubrick film. Kamuf writes:

> The scene of this haranguing lecture, which is titled with a nod to Nietzsche "Why Stephen King Writes Such Bad Novels," could feed the reader's speculation about one of the impulses channelling the terrific energy of *Memoirs*. Whoever has done time in the university under the charge of professing literature can no doubt recognise the urge to unleash a similar broadside attack on illusions cherished among a public of students force-fed their idea of "literature" by the bestseller industry.[61]

Kamuf allows that the distaste Acker shows in this scene can be appreciated, and even shared by the reader and potentially by Kamuf herself. However, Kamuf is instrumentally responsible for a broader interest in *The Shining* within critical theory—both in Kubrick's film, which could be considered art, and in King's novel, which, presumably, is in the dubious category of "best-seller." Her translation of *Specters of Marx* by Jacques Derrida popularized Derrida's term *hauntology*, a pun on "haunting" and "ontology"—the latter sounds almost indistinguishable from "hauntology" in Derrida's native French. The critical concept of *hauntology* was in turn instrumental to Fisher's 2007 reading of *The Shining*, a reading that rekindled interest in the text as a rich site for critical investigation. The title *Specters of Marx* comes from Marx's statement that "a spectre is haunting Europe, the spectre of communism."[62] Derrida takes this as his starting point and shows how risky it is to disavow the figure of the specter. There is a belief among those who uphold capitalist society, he writes, that "communism is finished since the collapse of the totalitarianisms of the twentieth century and not only is it finished, but it did not take place, it was only a ghost."

61 Peggy Kamuf, introduction to Du Plessis, *Memoirs*, xiv.
62 Karl Marx and Friedrich Engels, *The Communist Manifesto* (1848; London: Penguin, 2002), 1.

But those who believe this "do more than disavow the undeni-
able itself: a ghost never dies, it remains always to come and to
come-back."[63] The figure of the specter, according to Derrida,
is more powerful than a living figure. He goes on to describe
the practices that entire societies enact to disavow, repress, and
specifically conjure or exorcise a malignant force. As Kamuf elo-
quently translates:

> In the occult society of those who have sworn together [*des
> conjures*], certain subjects, either individual or collective,
> represent forces and ally themselves together in the name of
> common interests to combat a dreaded political adversary,
> that is, also to conjure it away. For to conjure means also to
> exorcise: to attempt to both destroy and to disavow a malig-
> nant, demonised, diabolised force, most often an evil-doing
> spirit, a spectre, a kind of ghost who comes back or who still
> risks coming back post mortem. Exorcism conjures away the
> evil in ways that are also irrational, using magical, mysteri-
> ous, even mystifying practices.[64]

Though this analysis relates to aggression against a political ad-
versary, it can also quite usefully describe any supernatural or
evil force, conspiracy, or cabal.

Conspiracy theories figure large in Rodney Ascher's 2012
documentary, *Room 237*. The film deals with super-fans of *The
Shining* and their fairly wild theories. Bill Blakemore, a writer
and actor, puts forward the thesis that the film version of *The
Shining* is a story about Native American genocide, a highly relevant hidden narrative for the Colorado-based story. His theory rests on the prop of Calumet baking soda cans that recur
throughout the film. The cans are decorated with an image of
a stereotypical Native American chief, and they are positioned

---

63 Jacques Derrida, *Specters of Marx: The State of the Debt, the Work of Mourning and the New International,* trans. Peggy Kamuf (1994; New York: Routledge, 2006), 123.

64 Ibid., 59.

at crucial moments in the film in ways that suggest an attempt to offer a narrative gloss. For example, in one scene where Jack is talking to the (un)dead Mr. Grady, the baking powder tin is directly behind Jack's head with the image of the peace pipe obscured, indicating that Native Americans' peace has been shattered. The opening scene of the documentary shows the poster for the 1981 UK release of *The Shining,* which states that the film is "the wave of terror that swept across America." Though this could be considered a typically hyperbolic presentation of a horror film, Blakemore argues in voice-over that there is also a hidden message in the poster: it speaks to the American imperial drive and the slaughter on which the new empire was founded. This narrowly focused claim does not address the multivalence of the text, but it does chime with my argument that the guilt of genocide haunts Colorado, going back to the Sand Creek massacre. Blakemore considers Grady's real, and Jack's attempted, murder of their families to be microcosmic versions of the Colorado genocide. Other contributors put forward various theories and readings. Perhaps the wildest claim in *Room 237* comes from Jay Weidner, who believes that the entire film serves only as a confession by Kubrick that the director staged the moon landings.[65] A more careful reading comes from Juli Kearns, who maps the impossible space of the Overlook to show how Kubrick intentionally uses camera tricks to mislead and disorient the viewer.[66] John Fell Ryan says of the practical cinematography: "They use the camera to create an emotional architecture in your mind, but at the same time [show] you that it is false. The set is so completely plastic that its contradictions pile up in your subconscious."[67] This is particularly relevant, as it

65 For more on this claim, see Jay Weidner, "Kubrick's Odessey" [sic], http://www.jayweidner.com/category/kubricks-odessey/

66 The maps can be seen at Juli Kearns, "Updated Maps of The Shining," *Idyllopus Press Presents* (blog), September 29, 2011, http://www.idyllopuspress.com/meanwhile/13834/updated-maps- of-the-shining.

67 For more on this perspective, see John Fell Ryan, "I Look at The Shining and It Shows Me Things: John Fell Ryan Gets Lost Inside the Overlook Hotel," *AdHoc,* May 22, 2012, http://adhoc.fm/post/john-fell-ryan-shining/.

contextualizes *The Shining* as plastic, malleable, and dangerous. The documentary reminds us that Kubrick sent a research team to Colorado for three months to uncover the real history of the state. There is no doubt that this was of serious interest to Kubrick and filtered into his version of King's story. In *The Shining*, no trace of Colorado history disappears.

This ghostly trace leaks from the basement, saturating the air, the house, and the deadly landscape. Luminol theory scratches straight through the palimpsest of history to reveal the accreted narratives below, from the basement where JonBenét was discovered to the originary genocide of the state of Colorado, where the Ramsey house rests uneasily on stolen and colonized land.

One Quantum of Light
Necrolight, Luminol

Every star in the universe will have burnt out, plunging the cosmos into a state of absolute darkness and leaving behind nothing but spent husks of collapsed matter. [...] Finally, in a state cosmologists call "asymptopia," the stellar corpses littering the empty universe will evaporate into a brief hailstorm of elementary particles.
— Raymond Brassier, *Nihil Unbound*

1. Necrolight

Three shepherds, the cousins Muhammed Ahmed el-Hamid, Jum'a Muhammed Khalil, and Khalil Musa, discovered the Dead Sea Scrolls serendipitously in the caves of Qumran in the West Bank in 1946. Named for their proximity to the Dead Sea, the scrolls contain the key to ancient languages, cultures, and narratives that were previously occulted. There were dangers associated with telling these stories, and the shepherds who discovered the scrolls risked their lives to reveal them to the world. They were unable to prove that they had discovered the scrolls legitimately, and feared that they might be accused of stealing them from a synagogue. In an uncanny doubling, the Nag Hammadi codices, comprising fifty-two Gnostic tractates, were found a year earlier, in 1945, in a sealed earthenware jar. The mother of one of the farmers who discovered the thirteen leather-bound papyrus scrolls, written in Coptic and translated from Greek, burned one of the books in its entirety and parts of a second book were destroyed.[1] These books were discovered in a mass grave, and are artifacts found at the scene of violence and death. This violence was overlaid palimpsestically with the later murder of six Coptic Christians on Christmas Eve, 2010, at the site of Nag Hammadi.[2] The murder was claimed to be in retaliation for the earlier rape of a twelve-year-old girl. The congruence of Christmas, the rape of a young girl, and murder reads like a gloss on the earlier murder of JonBenét. The story is subject to traumatic repetition; it is the return of the repressed.

The subjects of both the Dead Sea Scrolls and the Nag Hammadi codices are as uncannily bewitching as their respective discoveries: they speak of phantoms, apocalypse, repetition, and, ultimately, of the cadaver or the corpse, and they are documents from the crime scene. In his book *The Uncanny* Nicholas Royle

1 James VanderKam and Peter Flint, *The Meaning of the Dead Sea Scrolls: Their Significance for Understanding the Bible, Judaism, Jesus, and Christianity* (London: A&C Black, 2002), 4.

2 "Egypt Copts Killed in Christmas Church Attack," *BBC*, January 7, 2010, http://news.bbc.co.uk/1/hi/world/middle_east/8444851.stm.

describes one Nag Hammadi fragment as "a sort of futuristic ur-text for Abraham's account of the phantom, a strange figuring of what Derrida calls the *arrivant* ('a thinking of the past, a legacy that can come only from that which has not yet arrived')."[3] This unhierarchized approach to narrative immediacy that jumbles history ("ur-text"; "past") with future ("that which has not yet arrived"; "futuristic") to invoke the phantom text is broadened out to describe a larger phantom effect. This phantom effect relates not to the abjection of the cadaver, but to the absence of the corpse of Jesus, whose body is no longer legible:

> The various Gospel, Nag Hammadi and other accounts of seeing the dead Jesus alive again, together with the discovery of an empty tomb, constitute a testimony to what can be described, in Abraham's terms, as a vast phantom effect. Christian belief would be structured by the phantom effect of a figure whose reappearances beyond the grave, bolstered by the disappearance of his corpse, testify to unspoken or unspeakable secrets.[4]

Yet the empty tomb becomes a crime scene, a place where the absence of a corpse does not signify the absence of legibility. The empty tomb reproduced by the Nag Hammadi codices is a crime scene. The Qumran caves that inhabit the Israeli-occupied West Bank are crime scenes. The scrolls, which document these crime scenes, are the perfect subject for analysis with luminol theory for two reasons. First, they are apocalyptic or revelatory in nature; second, their true meaning is only accessible when forensic analysis of the papyrus scrolls using ultraviolet (UV) light, a blue chemical glow, is used to excavate layers of hidden narrative. The scrolls can only be read first by being unearthed, and then by being illuminated with blue light to slowly reveal hidden narratives. Dead Sea Scrolls scholars James VanderKam and Peter

---

3   Nicholas Royle, *The Uncanny* (Manchester: Manchester University Press, 2003), 285. Royle here quotes Derrida's *Specters of Marx*, 196, n. 39.

4   Royle, *The Uncanny*, 285.

Flint describe the use of UV light on the fragmentary scrolls: "As early as 1910, photography with ultraviolet light was being used on ancient documents. When a suitable ultraviolet source known as Wood's Lamp was invented in the 1920s, this method of reading manuscripts became common."[5] Although this technique allows for the excavation and illumination of hidden narratives, however, it also destroys the ink, deleting history as it is revealed: "Light can also affect the media used on papyrus. The inks on Egyptian papyri, being carbon black and red iron oxide, remain stable, but iron-gall ink, being an acidic product, ferric gallotannate, is less stable."[6] The chemical reaction between the ink on the papyrus and the ultraviolet light used to read it disintegrates and destabilizes narrative materially. The potential for damage when using luminol at a crime scene is high. Damage may occur not only physically, in the corrosive mechanism of the chemical reaction, but also in the potential for misreading, misdirection, and ellipses in understanding when false readings are provided, all of which can have material effects on both victims and suspects. Luminol theory similarly has both a generative and a destructive effect. It enables us to read buried histories, such as those found in the Dead Sea Scrolls, while corroding pre-existing, superficial narratives.

In modern English, the noun *apocalypse* and the related adjective *apocalyptic* have come to connote a catastrophe of cosmic proportions. So one speaks of the possibility of a nuclear apocalypse, or of the apocalyptic landscape of some futuristic films. It may come as something of a surprise, then, to learn that the underlying Greek word *apokalypsis* means simply "revelation" or "uncovering." The catastrophic connotations of the word come from its use in the last book of the New Testament, the Apocalypse, or Revelation of St. John.[7] Luminol theory aims

---

5   VanderKam and Flint, *The Meaning of the Dead Sea Scrolls,* 72.

6   Bridget Leach and John Tait, "Papyrus," in Paul T. Nicholson and Ian Shaw, *Ancient Egyptian Materials and Technology,* 226–53 (Cambridge: Cambridge University Press, 2000), 246.

7   John J. Collins, *Apocalypticism in the Dead Sea Scrolls* (London: Routledge, 1997), 1.

to reveal, and yet what it reveals is often catastrophic, deadly, and obscene.

The dead girl, unearthed, is excessive and reveals (produces an apocalypse of) what has been set out to be concealed (occulted) so she is more vital and vivid than ever, just as luminol on blood that is three years old produces a more intense glow than on fresh blood. The longer the dead girl is buried, the stronger her power is when she reanimates.

JonBenét's queer cousin, Jonbenet Blonde, a London-based drag queen, uses JonBenét's narrative as a political and aesthetic strategy and in so doing memorializes the dead girl. Just as Joyelle McSweeney suggests that Ryan Trecartin's work *I-Be Area* (2007) shows his characters "Wendy and Pasta […] look[ing] like decaying cheerleaders, like Laura Palmer had she stood up in the plastic to direct *Twin Peaks*,"[8] so too is Jonbenet Blonde like JonBenét Ramsey come back to autonomous life.[9] McSweeney writes about this kind of mystic transmutation in her discussion of the "loser occult." She argues:

> Loser occult envisions a kind of leveled, ambivalent, invisible perpetuity without precedence or antecedence, not based on permanence but on decay, infloration, contamination. It rejects youth, youthful promise, power, vigor, resonance, and shared experience but allows for the possibility of weird mutation, arbitrary reanimation, coincidence, corrosion, drag, and psychic twinship.[10]

---

8   Laura Palmer is a fictional character in David Lynch and Mark Frost's 1991–2017 television series *Twin Peaks* and also in the 1992 prequel film *Fire Walk With Me*. She was the catalyst for the show's events when the discovery of her body prompted an FBI investigation in the fictional town of Twin Peaks. The famous image of Laura Palmer, blue-white, and wrapped in plastic, is the symbol of the television series.

9   Joyelle McSweeney, *The Necropastoral: Poetry, Media, Occults* (Ann Arbor: University of Michigan Press, 2014), 154.

10 Ibid., 77.

Here the dead girl is electrified not by "youthful promise" and "vigor" but by "decay," "infloration," and "corrosion." The three dead women of *Memoirs,* JonBenét, Tiffany, and Kathy Acker, are subject to this "weird mutation," this "arbitrary reanimation," "drag," and absolute "psychic kinship," and Jonbenet Blonde, like Laura Palmer standing up in the plastic or like JonBenét lecturing at Boulder University, offers a creative, political queer strategy for memorializing the dead girl. In "loser occult" what is hidden will always proliferate, generate, and contaminate. This is a version of the return of the repressed that deals in spoliation as renewal and mutation as reproduction.

JonBenét suffered brutal rape and murder in her family home on Christmas morning, and this is an extreme and highly personal trauma. However, there are elements of her case that resonate with more universal lived experiences of gendered violence. In fact, these currents of trauma, violence, and gender flow equally through Du Plessis's fictional work and the true-crime coverage of the case. Perhaps there is little substantial difference between the rendering of the crime as creative nonfiction and as true crime. Du Plessis has appropriated and used the facts of a child's violent death to create a commercial, industrial product. However, he has also restructured the fabric of the case of JonBenét Ramsey into a new story, one that attempts to implicate an entire community and, by extension, a whole culture — including the reader and writer of the text — in the death and veneration of JonBenét Ramsey. There is an attempt at communion with marginalized and silenced voices that would be impossible in any other format.

2. Luminol

Mike Thompson's luminol lamp shines a light on human mortality and precarity.[11] The lamp is a sacred artifact, a cultic, ritual object that runs on human waste. The luminol lamp comprises a light bulb that is activated once human blood reacts with the luminol in the vial. This reaction, most commonly used to detect whether violence has taken place at suspected crime scenes, is taken out of context and given a magical twist by Thompson. The luminol lamp combines the human and the chemical. It invokes violence and disposability, but also transformation. Finally, it reminds us of the precarity of the human condition and the scarcity of the earth's resources by inviting the consumer to give a little of their own bodily fluid in exchange for light. Thompson dramatizes the danger of taking fuel for granted, and critiques patterns of consumption. The luminol lamp gives light, receives blood, explodes in chemical reaction, and regenerates waste fluid into energy. Thompson's luminol lamp combines organic and nonorganic matter and converts waste into aesthetic material, shining its queer unearthly light on human finitude.

Just as luminol releases one quantum of light when it comes into contact with biological material, so too does this book illuminate the memory of the dead women and girls who are its subject. This combination of the chemical and the occult is not accidental but rather illuminates the supernatural aspect that is presented by the luminosity of blood and, by extension, the awesome, numinous nature of scientific endeavor.

The fields of chemistry and biology are concerned with bioluminescence, and the subfield of forensic analysis is concerned more specifically with the potential properties of luminol that allow it to excavate hidden histories — the properties that enable forensic scientists to discover facts that can help them solve violent crimes. However, as with all scientific analyses, luminol evidence is unstable and can give false readings. Luminol glows

11 Rachael Rettner, "Lamp Runs on Human Blood," *LiveScience*, October 1, 2009, http://www.livescience.com/7920-lamp-runs-human-blood.html.

blue as it reacts with a range of biological and nonbiological materials, including "plant peroxidases (fresh potato juice), metals [...] and some cleaners (esp. hypochlorites.)"[12] Luminol has also been known to react with "an old porcelain sink or bathtub that has been exposed to cleaners."[13] The reaction between luminol and this range of materials, though, is never as intense. It produces a "'twinkling' or 'rippling' effect," whereas "luminol's reaction with a true bloodstain produces an intense, long-lasting, even glow, frequently in patterns such as spatters, smears, wipes, drag marks, or even footwear impressions."[14]

To categorize luminol theory as belonging to the sciences, even the social sciences, is to ignore the inherent subjectivity of literary theory. It is important to consider that this book does not simply deal with the reaction between certain kinds of organic matter. The difference between the "twinkling" effect of "fresh potato juice" and the intense "glow" of a room soaked with blood is not simply chemical. It relates to the lived — and dead — experience of those who have been subject to extreme violence. By reproducing the violence done to these bodies, I have engaged in a metapornographic investigation that does not exempt me from the charge of sexual exploitation that I aim to critique. Since the days of Victorian sexologist Richard von Krafft-Ebing, curators and cultural historians of pornography have been troubled by the question of whether pornographic representation stifles or generates coercive sexual practices. Lisa Downing recasts this disturbing question, framing it in relation to necrophiliac representation:

I would perhaps not go so far as to suggest that the line between a necrophiliac writer and a would-be practitioner is quite that thin, or that the equivalence between neurotic phantasy and acting out translates so literally and according to such a simple relation of cause and effect. Nonetheless, this idea sup-

---

12 James and Eckert, *Interpretation of Bloodstain Evidence at Crime Scenes,* 161.
13 Ibid.
14 Filippo Barni et al., "Forensic Application of the Luminol Reaction as a Presumptive Test for Latent Blood Detection," *Talanta* 72, no. 3 (2007): 908.

ports the persuasive view that literature serves a social function by encoding, within a safe space, desires which must not be enacted in the world. However, the fear exists, as Krafft-Ebing has made clear, that such textual representation may simultaneously defuse and stimulate the impulse. This reaches the heart of contemporary debates on pornography, which question how far it is safe (and indeed helpful) to diffuse images and fantasies that facilitate sexual release, thereby possibly reducing the incidence of coercive sexual acts.[15]

By engaging in metapornographic enquiry in this book I cannot exempt myself from this morally sticky position. I offer two counterpoints: First, I agree with Peter Brooks that — in Elisabeth Bronfen's paraphrasing — "all narrative may well be obituary in that it seeks a retrospective knowledge that comes after the end, which in human terms places it on the far side of death."[16] And, I also offer the hope, in an attempt to ameliorate this necessarily complicit position, that nowhere are the hidden stories of this book more palpable and more immediate than when doused in blood. The murdered and mutilated bodies that appear in the pages of this book are reclaimed as autonomous bodies and voices that speak from the margins, from beyond the pleasure principle.

---

15 Downing, *Desiring the Dead,* 62–63.
16 Bronfen, *Over Her Dead Body,* 61.

Each blood-soaked body produces its own "intense, long-lasting, even glow" that cannot be doused or even transmuted. As the bodies of these dead girls "decay" there will always be "one quantum of light" emitted in their memory.

Bibliography

Acker, Kathy. "Dead Doll Humility." *Postmodern Culture* 1, no.
　1 (1990). http://pmc.iath.virginia.edu/text-only/issue.990/
　acker.990.

Albrecht, H. O. "Über die Chemiluminescenz des Aminoph-
　thalaurehydrazids." *Zeitschrift für Physikalische Chemie* 136
　(1928): 321–30.

Bachelard, Gaston. *The Poetics of Space.* Translated by Maria
　Jolas. New York: Penguin Classics, 2014.

Balko, Radley. "A Brief History of Forensics." *Washington Post.*
　April 21, 2015.

Barni Filippo et al. "Forensic Application of the Luminol
　Reaction as a Presumptive Test for Latent Blood Detection."
　Talanta 72, no. 3 (2007): 908.

Bernheimer, Charles and Claire Kahane, eds. *In Dora's Case:
　Freud—Hysteria—Feminism,* 2nd ed. New York: Columbia
　University Press, 1990.

Bersani, Leo. *The Culture of Redemption.* Cambridge: Harvard
　University Press, 1990.

Best, Stephen and Sharon Marcus. "Surface Reading: An Intro-
　duction." Representations 108, no. 1 (2009): 1–21.

Blau DuPlessis, Rachel. *Writing beyond the Ending: Narrative
　Strategies of Twentieth-Century Women Writers.* Blooming-
　ton: Indiana University Press, 1985.

Bond, Henry. *Lacan at the Scene.* Cambridge: MIT Press, 2009.

Brassier, Raymond. *Nihil Unbound.* London: Palgrave. 2007.

Bronfen, Elisabeth. *Over Her Dead Body: Death, Femininity
　and the Aesthetic.* Manchester: Manchester University Press,
　1992.

Brooks, Peter. *Reading for the Plot: Design and Intention in Narrative.* Cambridge: Harvard University Press, 1992.

Butler, Judith. *Bodies That Matter: On the Discursive Limits of Sex.* 1993; New York: Routledge, 2011.

———. *Gender Trouble: Feminism and the Subversion of Identity,* 2nd ed. 1990; New York: Routledge, 2006.

Caruth, Cathy. *Unclaimed Experience.* Baltimore: John Hopkins Press, 1996.

Céline, Louis-Ferdinand. *L'Ecole des cadavres.* Paris: Denoël, 1938.

Coles, Bryony, John Coles, and Mogens Schou Jørgensen. *Bog Bodies, Sacred Sites, and Wetland Archaeology.* Exeter: Wetland Archaeology Research Project, 1999.

Collins, John J. *Apocalypticism in the Dead Sea Scrolls.* London: Routledge, 1997.

"Colorado Bureau of Investigation Cold Case File: Julie L. Cunningham." https://apps.colorado.gov/apps/coldcase/casedetail.html?id=2421.

"Combined DNA Index System." FBI. https://www.fbi.gov/about-us/lab/biometric-analysis/codis/combined-dna-index-system%20.

Creed, Barbara. *The Monstrous-Feminine: Film, Feminism, Psychoanalysis.* London: Routledge, 1993.

Croft Boyd, Louie. "The Tuberculosis Situation in Denver, Colorado." *American Journal of Nursing* 7, no. 4 (1907): 265–68.

Cronk, Olivia. *Skin Horse.* Notre Dame: Action Books, 2012.

Cullen, Dave. *Columbine.* London: Old Street Publishing, 2009.

Derrida, Jacques. "Hostipitality." Translated by Barry Stocker with Forbes Morlock. *Angelaki* 5, no. 3 (2000): 3–18.

———. *Specters of Marx: The State of the Debt, the Work of Mourning and the New International.* Translated by Peggy Kamuf. 1994; New York: Routledge, 2006.

Don Ihde. *Hermeneutic Phenomenology: The Philosophy of Paul Ricœur.* Evanston: Northwestern University Press, 1971.

Douglas, Mary. *Purity and Danger: An Analysis of the Concepts of Pollution and Taboo.* 1966; London: Routledge, 2002.

Downing, Lisa. *Desiring the Dead: Necrophilia and Nineteenth-Century French Literature*. Oxford: Legenda, 2003.

Du Plessis, Michael. *The Memoirs of JonBenet Ramsey by Kathy Acker*. Los Angeles: Les Figues Press, 2012.

Edelman, Lee. *No Future: Queer Theory and the Death Drive*. Durham: Duke University Press, 2004.

"Egypt Copts Killed in Christmas Church Attack." *BBC*. January 7, 2010. http://news.bbc.co.uk/1/hi/world/middle_east/8444851.stm.

Faber, Toby. *Fabergé's Eggs: One Man's Masterpieces and the End of an Empire*. London: Pan, 2009.

Fell Ryan, John. "I Look at *The Shining* and It Shows Me Things: John Fell Ryan Gets Lost Inside the Overlook Hotel." *AdHoc*. May 22, 2012. http://adhoc.fm/post/john-fell-ryan-shining/.

Felman, Shoshana. *Testimony: Crises of Witnessing in Literature, Psychoanalysis, History*. London and New York: Routledge, 1992.

Fisher, Mark. "You Have Always Been the Caretaker: The Spectral Spaces of the Overlook Hotel." *Perforations* 29 (2007). http://www.pd.org/Perforations/perf29/mf1.pdf.

Foster, Hal. *The Return of the Real: The Avant-Garde at the End of the Century*. Cambridge: MIT Press, 1996.

Foucault, Michel. *Language, Counter-Memory, Practice: Selected Essays and Interviews*. Edited by Donald F. Bouchard. Ithaca: Cornell University Press, 1980.

——. *The Archaeology of Knowledge*. Translated by A.M. Sheridan Smith. 1972; London: Routledge, 2002.

Franklin, James. *The Science of Conjecture: Evidence and Probability before Pascal*. Baltimore: Johns Hopkins University Press, 2001.

Freud, Sigmund. *Beyond the Pleasure Principle and Other Writings*. London: Penguin, 2003.

——. *The "Wolfman" and Other Cases*. Translated by Louise Adey Huish. London: Penguin Classics, 2002.

——. *Three Case Histories*. 1963; New York: Touchstone, 2008.

Gagnier, Regenia. *Subjectivities: A History of Self-Representation in Britain, 1832–1920.* New York: Oxford University Press, 1991.

Galton, Francis. *Essays in Eugenics,* 3rd ed. 1909; CreateSpace Independent Publishing Platform, 2013.

———. "Eugenics: Its Definition, Scope, and Aims." *American Journal of Sociology* 10, no. 1 (1904): 1–25.

———. *Finger Prints.* 1892; Amherst: Prometheus Books, 2006.

Garrison, Daniel. "The 'Locus Inamoenus': Another Part of the Forest." *Arion* 2, no. 1 (1992): 98–114.

Gilbert, Sandra M. and Susan Gubar. *The Madwoman in the Attic: The Woman Writer and the Nineteenth-Century Literary Imagination,* 2nd ed. New Haven: Yale University Press, 2000.

Göransson, Johannes. *Entrance to a Colonial Pageant in Which We All Begin to Intricate.* Grafton: Tarpaulin Sky Press, 2011.

Grayson, Donald K. "Donner Party Deaths: A Demographic Assessment." *Journal of Anthropological Research* 46, no. 3 (1990): 223–42.

Grispino, R.R. "The Effect of Luminol on the Serological Analysis of Dried Human Bloodstains." *Crime Laboratory Digest* 17, no. 1 (1990): 13–23.

Hoffman, Calvin. *The Murder of the Man Who Was "Shakespeare."* 1955; New York: Grosset & Dunlap, 1960.

Hughes, Ted. *Tales from Ovid: Twenty-Four Passages from the "Metamorphoses."* London: Faber & Faber, 1997.

Hughey, Matthew W. "Cinethetic Racism: White Redemption and Black Stereotypes in 'Magical Negro' Films." *Social Problems* 56, no. 3 (2009): 543–77.

Huntress, Ernest, Lester Stanley, and Almon Parker. "The Preparation of 3-Aminophthalhydrazide for Use in the Demonstration of Chemiluminescence." *Journal of the American Chemical Society* 56, no. 1 (1934): 241–42.

James, Stuart H. and William G. Eckert. *Interpretation of Bloodstain Evidence at Crime Scenes,* 2nd ed. Boca Raton: CRC Press, 1998.

"Jonbenet Ramsey: Who Killed Jonbenet," Mills Productions. Channel 4. 1998. http://www.millsproductions.co.uk/jonbenet-ramsey/who-killed-jonbenet.shtml.

King, Stephen. *The Shining.* 1977; London: Hodder Paperbacks, 2011.

Knights, L.C. *How Many Children Had Lady MacBeth? An Essay in the Theory and Practice of Shakespeare Criticism.* Cambridge: Gordon Fraser, Minority Press, 1933.

Kristeva, Julia. *Powers of Horror: An Essay on Abjection.* Translated by Leon S. Roudiez. New York: Columbia University Press, 1982.

Kroker, Arthur. *Panic Encyclopedia.* New York: St. Martin's Press, 1989.

Lacan, Jacques. "The Mirror-Phase as Formative of the Function of the I." *New Left Review* 51 (1968): 71–77.

Larkin, Ralph W. "The Columbine Legacy: Rampage Shootings as Political Acts." *American Behavioral Scientist* 52, no. 9 (2009): 1309–26.

Laux, D.L. "Effects of Luminol on the Subsequent Analysis of Bloodstains." *Journal of Forensic Sciences* 36, no. 5 (1991): 1512–20.

Lewis, Shanna. "How Tuberculosis Fueled Colorado's Growth." *Colorado Matters.* February 10, 2015. http://www.cpr.org/news/story/how-tuberculosis-fueled-colorados-growth.

Leys, Ruth. *Trauma: A Genealogy.* Chicago: University of Chicago Press, 2000.

Luckhurst, Roger. *The Trauma Question.* London and New York: Routledge, 2013.

Lucretius. *On the Nature of Things.* Translated by W.H.D. Rouse, rev. Martin F. Smith. 1924; Cambridge: Harvard University Press, 1975.

Lynch, Jack. *Deception and Detection in Eighteenth-Century Britain.* Aldershot: Ashgate, 2008.

Maas, Peter. *In a Child's Name: The Legacy of a Mother's Murder.* New York: Simon and Schuster, 1990.

Malabou, Catherine. *Plasticity at the Dusk of Writing: Dialectic, Destruction, Deconstruction.* New York: Columbia, 2009.

Marcus, Sharon. *Between Women: Friendship, Desire, and Marriage in Victorian England*. Princeton: Princeton University Press, 2007.

Marder, Elissa. *The Mother in the Age of Mechanical Reproduction: Psychoanalysis, Photography, Deconstruction*. New York: Fordham University Press, 2012.

Marx, Karl and Friedrich Engels. *The Communist Manifesto*. 1848; London: Penguin, 2002.

McMenamin, *Gerald R. Forensic Linguistics: Advances in Forensic Stylistics*. Boca Raton: CRC Press, 2002.

McSweeney, Joyelle. "Can the Necropastoral Be Political?" *Montevidayo*. January 31, 2011. http://www.montevidayo.com/can-the-necropastoral-be-political.

———. *The Necropastoral*. Arizona: Spork Press, 2011.

———. *The Necropastoral: Poetry, Media, Occults*. Ann Arbor: University of Michigan Press, 2014.

Michasiw, Kim Ian. *American Gothic: New Interventions in a National Narrative*. Edited by Robert K. Martin and Eric Savoy. Iowa City: University of Iowa Press, 1998.

Miller, D.A. *Narrative and Its Discontents: Problems of Closure in the Traditional Novel*. Princeton: Princeton University Press, 1981.

———. *The Novel and the Police*. Berkeley: University of California Press, 1988.

Morrison, Toni. *The Bluest Eye*. 1970; London: Vintage, 1999.

Morton, Timothy. *The Ecological Thought*. Cambridge: Harvard University Press, 2012.

Murphy, Bernice M. *The Suburban Gothic in American Popular Culture*. Basingstoke: Palgrave, 2009.

Nicholson, Paul T. and Ian Shaw. *Ancient Egyptian Materials and Technology*. Cambridge: Cambridge University Press, 2000.

Ovid. *Metamorphoses: A New Verse Translation*. Translated by David Raeburn. London: Penguin Classics, 2004.

———. *Metamorphoses*. Translated by A.D. Melville. Oxford: Oxford Paperbacks, 1998.

Pollack, Andrew. "DNA Evidence Can Be Fabricated, Scientists Show." *New York Times.* August 17, 2009. http://www.nytimes.com/2009/08/18/science/18dna.html

Rainwater, Don and Kellie Rainwater. *The Dark Side of Colorado: Murder, Mayhem, and Massacre.* CreateSpace Independent Publishing Platform, 2008.

Reagan, Charles E. *Paul Ricœur: His Life and His Work.* Chicago: University of Chicago Press, 1996.

Rettner, Rachael. "Lamp Runs on Human Blood." *LiveScience.* October 1, 2009. http://www.livescience.com/7920-lamp-runs-human-blood.html.

Richlin, Amy. *Pornography and Representation in Greece and Rome.* New York: Oxford University Press, 1992.

Ricœur Paul. *Freud and Philosophy.* Translated by Denis Savage. New Haven: Yale University Press, 1970.

Roger Luckhurst, *The Shining.* London: BFI Classics, 2013.

Royle, Nicholas. *The Uncanny.* Manchester: Manchester University Press, 2003.

Scott-Baumann, Alison. *Ricœur and the Hermeneutics of Suspicion.* London: Continuum, 2009.

Segal, Charles. *Landscape in Ovid's Metamorphoses: A Study in the Transformations of a Literary Symbol.* Wiesbaden: F. Steiner Verlag, 1969.

Specht, W. "The Chemiluminescence of Hemin: An Aid for Finding and Recognizing Blood Stains Important for Forensic Purposes." *Angewante Chemie* 50 (1937): 155–57.

Spooner, Catherine and Emma McEvoy. T*he Routledge Companion to Gothic.* Abingdon: Routledge, 2007.

Stewart, Susan. *Crimes of Writing: Problems in the Containment of Representation.* Durham: Duke University Press, 1994.

Sweet, Paige. "Where's the Booty? The Stakes of Textual and Economic Piracy as Seen through the Work of Kathy Acker." *darkmatter* 5 (2009). http://www.darkmatter101.org/site/2009/12/20/where%E2%80%99s-the-booty-the-stakes-of-textual-and-economic-piracy-as-seen-through-the-work-of-kathy-acker/.

"The Francis Galton Papers." *Wellcome Library.* http://well-comelibrary.org/collections/digital-collections/makers-of-modern-genetics/digitised-archives/francis-galton/.

Thornton, John I. and Ralph S. Maloney. "The Chemistry of the Luminol Reaction—Where To from Here?" *California Association of Criminalists Newsletter.* September 1985, 9–17.

Twining, William. *Rethinking Evidence: Exploratory Essays.* Evanston: Northwestern University Press, 1990.

VanderKam, James and Peter Flint. *The Meaning of the Dead Sea Scrolls: Their Significance for Understanding the Bible, Judaism, Jesus, and Christianity.* London: A&C Black, 2002.

Williamson, Kenneth L. *Macroscale and Microscale Organic Experiments,* 4th ed. Boston: Houghton Mifflin, 2005.

Wyndham, John. *The Midwich Cuckoos.* London: Penguin, 2008.